SEVEN GRAMMARS OF THE DIALECTS AND SUBDIALECTS OF THE BIHĀRĪ LANGUAGE

SEVEN

GRAMMARS

OF THE DIALECTS AND SUBDIALECTS
OF THE

BIHÁRÍ LANGUAGE

SPOKEN IN THE PROVINCE OF BIHÁR, IN THE EASTERN PORTION OF THE NORTH-WESTERN PROVINCES, AND IN THE NORTHERN PORTION OF THE CENTRAL PROVINCES

(Volume-2 in Two Parts)

Part-4. Máithil Bhojpúrí Dialect
Part-5. South Máithilí Dialect

George A. Grierson, BC.S.

Publications

KALPAZ PUBLICATIONS
DELHI-110 052

Seven Grammars of the Dialects and Subdialects of the Bihárí Language

ISBN : 81-7835-451-9 (Set)
ISBN : 81-7835-453-5 (Vol. 2)

Published in 2005 in India by
Kalpaz Publications,
C-30, Satyawati Nagar,
Delhi-110 052
E-mail : kalpaz@hotmail.com

Laser Typesetting at: Tact Computer Graphics, Delhi
Printed at: Salasar Imaging System, Delhi

SEVEN

GRAMMARS

OF THE DIALECTS AND SUBDIALECTS OF THE

BIHÁRÍ LANGUAGE.

SPOKEN IN THE PROVINCE OF BIHÁR, IN THE EASTERN PORTION OF THE NORTH-WESTERN PROVINCES, AND IN THE NORTHERN PORTION OF THE CENTRAL PROVINCES.

PART IV.

MAITHIL-BHOJPÚRÍ DIALECT

OF CENTRAL AND SOUTH MUZAFFARPÚR.

Compiled under orders of the Government of Bengal

By GEORGE A. GRIERSON, B.C.S.,

OFFG. JOINT-MAGISTRATE OF PATNA.

CALCUTTA:

PRINTED AT THE BENGAL SECRETARIAT PRESS.

1884

CONTENTS.

DIVISION III.

INDECLINABLES.

APPENDIX I.

SELECTIONS IN THE CENTRAL MUZAFFARPÚR DIALECT.

APPENDIX II.

NOTE ON THE USE OF THE VARIOUS VERBAL TERMINATIONS.

INTRODUCTION

§ 1. The following Grammar treats of the dialect spoken in Central and South Muzaffarpúr. It is principally composed of South Maithilí forms, but is largely impregnated with Bhojpúrí forms, especially in the west of the district. In this Grammar the dialect of the eastern portion of the tract is treated as the standard, the peculiarities of the more western language being generally given in footnotes.

§ 2. The alphabet and rules for spelling will be found in the General Introduction to this series of Grammars, and the remarks therein found are not repeated here.

DIVISION I.

DECLENSION.

CHAPTER I.

NOUNS.

§ 3. For general remarks, see the General Introduction, § 38 and ff.

The following are the post-positions used in declining the noun in this dialect :—

		Power.
Nom.	*Wanting.*	
Acc.	*Wanting* or के *ke.*	
Instr.	से *se.*	'By.'
Dat.	के *ke.*	'To.'
	ला *lá,* लेल *lel.*	'For.'
Abl.	से *se.*	'From.'
Gen.	के *kĕ.*	'Of.'
Loc.	में *mẽ.*	'In.'
Voc.	*Wanting.*	

All these post-positions will only be used in one example, that of घोड़ा *ghoṛá,* 'a horse ;' but they can all be used with all nouns.

Except that for the genitive, they can be used with all pronouns. In the genitive singular many pronouns do not take this post-position, but have other forms subject to special rules.

The following are examples of declension.

§ 4. (a) Masculine Tadbhavas in आ *á*.

Example of the declension of a *tadbhava* * masculine noun in आ *á* :–

घोड़ा *ghoṛá*, 'a horse.'

Short form, { Weak, घोड़ *ghoṛ*. Strong, घोड़ा *ghoṛá*. } Long form,* घोड़वा *ghŏṛ'wá*. Redundant form,† घोड़ौवा *ghŏṛauwá*.

Singular.

Nom.	घोड़ा [1] *ghoṛá*,	'a horse.'
Acc.	घोड़ा *ghoṛá* or घोड़ा के *ghoṛá ke*,	'a horse.'
Instr.	घोड़ा से *ghoṛá se*,	'by a horse.'
Dat.	घोड़ा के *ghoṛá ke*, or ला *lá*, or लेल *lel*,	'to' *or* 'for a horse.'
Abl.	घोड़ा से, *ghoṛá se*,	'from a horse.'
Gen.	घोड़ा कें [2] *ghoṛá kĕ*,	'of a horse.'
Loc.	घोड़ा में *ghoṛá mẽ*,	'in a horse.'
Voc.	हे घोड़ा *he ghoṛá* !	'O horse!'

[1] Or घोड़ *ghoṛ*, घोड़वा *ghŏṛ'wá*, or घोड़ौवा *ghŏṛauwá*, and so throughout the singular.

[2] The genitival affix कें *kĕ* remains unchanged before all genders and cases. In Western Muzaffarpúr, however, the Bhojpúrí practice is followed of using कें *kĕ* before nouns in the nominative and का *ká* before nouns in an oblique case.

Plural.

Nom.	घोड़न [1] *ghoṛan*,	'horses.'
Acc.	घोड़न *ghoṛan*, घोड़न के *ghoṛan ke*,	'horses.'
Instr.	घोड़न से *ghoṛan se*,	'by horses.'
Dat.	घोड़न के *ghoṛan ke*, or ला *lá*, or लेल *lel*,	'to' *or* 'for horses.'
Abl.	घोड़न से *ghoṛan se*,	'from horses.'
Gen.	घोड़न कें [2] *ghoṛan kĕ*,	'of horses.'
Loc.	घोड़न में *ghoṛan mẽ*,	'in horses.'
Voc.	हे घोड़न *he ghoṛan* !	'O horses!'

[1] Or घोड़वन *ghŏṛ'wan* or घोड़ौवन *ghŏṛauwan*, and so throughout the plural.

[2] See note [2] to singular.

---

* See General Introduction, § 12. † See General Introduction, §§ 12, 38, and ff.

§ 5. (b) Masculine Nouns ending in Silent Consonants.

Example of the declension of a masculine noun ending in a silent consonant:—

घर *ghar*, 'a house.'

Short form, घर *ghar*. Long form,* घरवा *ghar'wá*. Redundant form,* घरौवा *gharauwá*.

Singular.

Nom.	घर[1] *ghar,*	'a house.'
Acc.	घर, घर के *ghar, ghar ke,*	'a house.'
Instr.	घरैं *gharẽ,* घर से *ghar se,*	'by a house.'
Dat.	घर के *ghar ke,*	'to a house.'
Abl.	घर से *ghar se,*	'from a house.'
Gen.	घर कै *ghar kĕ,*	'of a house.'
Loc.	घरे *ghare,* घर मेँ *ghar mẽ,*	'in a house.'
Voc.	हे घर *he ghar !*	'O house !'

[1] Or घरवा *ghar'wá,* घरौवा *gharauwá,* and so throughout the singular

Plural.

Nom.	घरन[1] *gharan,*	'houses.'
Acc.	घरन *gharan* or घरन के *gharan ke,*	'houses.'
Instr.	घरन से *gharan se,*	'by houses.'
Dat.	घरन के *gharan ke,*	'to' *or* 'for houses.'
Abl.	घरन से *gharan se,*	'from houses.'
Gen.	घरन कै *gharan kĕ,*	'of houses.'
Loc.	घरन मेँ *gharan mẽ,*	'in houses.'
Voc.	हे घरन *he gharan !*	'O houses !'

[1] Or घरवन *ghar'wan,* घरौवन *gharauwan,* and so throughout the plural.

§ 6. It is not necessary to decline further any nouns in full, as the above examples suffice. All nouns ending in vowels are declined like घोड़ा *ghoṛá*, and all those ending in silent consonants like घर *ghar*. The final

* See General Introduction, §§ 12, 38, and ff.

syllables of all long and redundant forms may optionally be nasalized by the addition of *anunásik :* thus घोड़वा *ghŏṛ'wá* or घोड़वाँ *ghŏṛ'wá̃ ;* घरौवा *gharauwá* or घरौवाँ *gharauwá̃ ;* मलिया *maliyá* or मलियाँ *maliyá̃*.

NOTE, however, that—

(1) Occasionally in the case of masculine nouns ending in a silent consonant we find an instrumental in ऐं *ẽ* and a locative in ए *e :* thus हम बलेँ ले जाएब *ham balẽ le jáĕb*, 'I shall take away by force,' where बलेँ *balẽ* is the instrumental of बल *bal*, 'force;' घाटे *gháṭe*, 'at a landing stage,' locative of घाट *gháṭ*, 'a landing stage:' so also घरे घरे *ghare ghare*, 'in every house,' 'from house to house.'

(2) All nouns ending in a long vowel shorten it before the plural termination न *n :* thus घोड़न *ghoṛan* from घोड़ा *ghoṛá*.

(3) Certain verbal nouns ending in ल *l* have an oblique form in ला *lá :* thus देखल *dekhal*, abl. देखला से *dĕkh'lá se*, 'from seeing;' also verbal nouns in the form of the root have an oblique form in ए *ĕ :* thus देख *dekh*, dat. देखे के *dekhĕ ke* 'for seeing.' Full particulars concerning these nouns will be found in § 111.

An example of each of the more common forms of nouns follows :—

§ 7. (c) Masculine Tatsamas* in आ *á*.

राजा *rája*, 'a king.'

Short form, राजा *rájá*. Long form,* रजवा *raj'wá*. Redundant form,* रजौवा *rajauwá*.

Gen. sing. राजा के *rájá kĕ*.
Nom. plur. राजन *rájan*.

---

* See General Introduction, §§ 12, 38, and ff., 34 and 36.

§ 8. (d) Masculine Nouns in ई *í*.

माली *málí*, 'a gardener.'

Short form, माली *málí*. Long form,* मलिया *maliyá*. Redundant form,* मलियवा *maliyawá* or मलीवा *malíwá*.

Gen. sing. माली के *málí kĕ*.
Nom. plur. मालिन *málin*.

§ 9. (e) Masculine Nouns in ऊ *ú*.

नाऊ *náú*, 'a barber.'†

Short form, नाऊ *náú*. Long form,‡ नउआ *naüá* or नौआ *nauá*. Redundant form,‡ नउअवा *naüawá* or नौअवा *nauawá*.

Gen. sing. नाऊ के *náú kĕ*.
Nom. plur. नाउन *náün*.

§ 10. (f) Feminine Nouns in ई *í*.

पोथी *pothí*, 'a book.'

Short form, पोथी *pothí*. Long form,‡ पोथिया *pŏthiyá*. Redundant form,‡ पोथियवा *pŏthiyawá* or पोथीवा *pothíwá*.

Gen. sing. पोथी के *pothí kĕ*.
Nom. plur. पोथिन, *pothin*.

---

* See General Introduction, §§ 12, 38, and ff., 34 and 36.

† Kellogg in his Hindí Grammar incorrectly gives आँसू *ású* as an example of a feminine noun in ऊ *ú*: it is masculine. आँसू *ású* is not used in Bihárí, लोर *lor* being the word for 'a tear.'

‡ See General Introduction, §§ 12, 38, and ff., and 34 to 36.

§ 11. (g) Feminine Nouns ending in a Silent Consonant.

बात *bát*, 'a word.'

Short form, बात *bát*. Long form,* बतिया *batiyá*. Redundant form,* बतियवा *batiyawá* or बतीवा *batíwa*.

Acc. sing. बात के *bát ke*.
Gen. sing. बात के *bát kĕ*.
Nom. plur. बातन *bátan*.

§ 12. Periphrastic Plural.

With reference to the above plural forms, it must be noted that every noun can also form a periphrastic plural by the addition of a word signifying plurality, such as सभ *sabh*, 'all;' or, in the case of *rational* beings, such as लोग *log*, 'people.' Example: घर सभ *ghar sabh* instead of घरन *gharan*, and माली लोग *málí log* for मालिन *málin*. Sometimes even this plural affix is omitted, so that a plural noun appears under a singular form. An example occurs in the ninth of the following sentences, where बेटा *beṭá* is used for बेटा सभ *beṭá sabh*. This is the regular rule when a numeral adjective precedes, as in Nos. 6 and 7 of the following sentences. Sometimes these plural affixes are added pleonastically to a word already in the plural form, *e.g.* पोथिन सभ *pothin sabh* for पोथिन *pothin*.

§ 13. Genitival Affixes.

The following examples have been specially designed to exhibit the use of the genitival affixes. Each sentence is given as spoken (*a*) in Eastern and (*b*) in Western Muzaffarpúr:—

1. (*a*) ई राजा के मन्दिर छिकैन्ह. 'This is the king's temple.'
Í rájá kĕ mandir chhikainh.
(*b*) ई राजा के मन्दिर बटैन्ह.
Í rájá kĕ mandir baṭainh.

* See General Introduction, §§ 12, 38, and ff., and 34 and 36.

2.	(*a*) हम कन्स के लौँड़ी छी. *Ham Kans kĕ lãuṛi chhi.*	'I am the maid-servant of King Kans.'
	(*b*) हम कन्स के दासी बटिऐन्ह. *Ham Kans kĕ dási baṭiainh.*	
3.	(*a*) मध॰माँछी के झूँड़ उड़ गेलैक. *Madh'măchhi kè jhũṛ uṛ gĕlaik.*	'A swarm of bees flew away.'
	(*b*) मधुमाखी के झूँड़ उड़ गेल. *Madhumákhi kĕ jhũṛ uṛ gel.*	
4.	(*a*) कप॰टी के मार॰ला मेँ दोख नहिँ कौनो. *Kap'ṭi kĕ már'lá mẽ dokh nahĩ kaunŏ.*	'There is no sin in slaying a deceiver.'
	(*b*) कप॰टी का मार॰ला के कुछ दोख नठ. *Kap'ṭi ká már'lá kè kuchh dokh na.*	
5.	(*a*) मथुरा के मौँगी सभ कनैत चल गेल॰थिन्ह. *Mathurá kĕ mãugi sabh kanait chal gĕl'thinh.*	'The women of Mathurá departed weeping.'
	(*b*) मथुरा के नारी सभ रोऐत चल गेलिन. *Mathurá kĕ nári sabh rŏait chal gelin.*	
6.	(*a*) कै रङ्ग के बात सुनल गेल. *Kai raṅg kĕ bat sunal gel.*	'Matters of many kinds were heard.'
	(*b*) बहुत तरह के बात सुनल गेल. *Bahut tarah kĕ bát sunal gel.*	
7.	(*a*) स्फटिक के चार फाटक टूट गेलै. *Sphaṭik kĕ chár pháṭak ṭúṭ gĕlai.*	'Four gates of crystal broke.'
	(*b*) स्फटिक के चार फाटक टूट गेल. *Sphaṭik kĕ chár pháṭak ṭúṭ gel.*	
8.	(*a & b*) देस देस के राजा ऐलन्ह. *Des des kĕ rájá ailanh.*	'Kings of all countries came.'

9. (*a*) ऊ सभ माली के बेटा छतन्ह.
Ú sabh máli ké betá chhatanh.
'They are the sons of the gardener.'

(*b*) ऊ सभ माली के बेटा हतन.
Ú sabh máli kĕ betá hatan.

10. (*a*) हम राजा के गाँव में ऐली.
Ham rájá kĕ gãw mẽ ailí.
'I came into the king's villages.'

(*b*) हम राजा का गौँवन में ऐली.
Ham rájá ká gãwan mĕ aili.

11. (*a*) पण्डितन के घर में कइ रङ्ग के पोथी छैन्ह.
Panditan kĕ ghar mẽ kaï rang kĕ pothi chainh.
'There are many books in *pandits'* houses.'

(*b*) पण्डित सभ का घर में बहुत पोथी बटैन्ह.
Pandit sabh ká ghar mẽ bahut pothi batainh.

CHAPTER II.

ADJECTIVES.

§ 14. Gender.

See General Introduction, § 42 and ff.

§ 15. Numeral Adjectives.

The cardinals are nearly the same as those in High Hindí. The following are the ones that present points of difference :—

1 = एक *ĕk.*
2 = दू *dú.*
6 = छव *chhaw.*
11 = इगारह *igárah.*
15 = पन॰रह *pan'rah.*
16 = सोरह *sorah.*
21 = एकैस *ĕkais.*
31 = एक॰तिस *ĕk'tis.*
32 = बत्तिस *battis.*
33 = तैँतिस *tẽtis.*
34 = चौँतिस *chaũtis.*
35 = पैँतिस *pãĩtis.*
36 = छत्तिस *chhattis.*
37 = सैँतिस *sãĩtis.*
38 = अड़॰तिस *aṛ'tis.*
39 = उन॰तालिस *un'tális.*
40 = चालिस *chális.*
41 = एक॰तालिस *ĕk'tális.*
42 = बेआलिस *bĕális.*
43 = तैँतालिस *tĕ̃tális.*
44 = चवालिस *chawális.*
45 = पैँतालिस *pãĩtális.*
46 = छियालिस *chhiyális.*
47 = सैँतालिस *sãĩtális.*
48 = अड़॰तालिस *aṛ'tális.*
54 = चौवन *chauwan.*
64 = चौसठ *chausaṭh.*
66 = छियासठ *chhiyásaṭh.*
67 = सर॰सठ *sar'saṭh.*
74 = चौहत्तर *chauhattar.*
82 = बेआसी *bĕásí.*
84 = चौरासी *chaŭrásí.*
86 = छियासी *chhiyásí.*
94 = चौरानबे *chaŭránawe.*
96 = छियानबे *chhiyánawe.*
100 = सै *sai.*

§ 16. Ordinals.

The ordinals up to 'sixth' are as follows:—

1st = पहिल *pahil ; obl.* पहिला *pahilá* or पहला *pah'lá.**
2nd = दोसर *dosar ; obl.* दोसरा *dŏs'rá.**
3rd = तेसर *tesar ; obl.* तेसरा *tĕs'rá.**
4th = चौठ *chauṭh.*
5th = पँचवाँ *pãch'wã* or पाँचम *pãcham.*
6th = छठवाँ *chhaṭh'wã* or छठम *chhaṭham.*

The ordinals above 'sixth' are all formed by adding वाँ *wã* or म *m* to the cardinals : as दसवाँ *das'wã* or दसम *dasam*, 'tenth;' पचसवाँ *pachas'wã* or पचासम *pachásam*, 'fiftieth'

§ 17. Fractional Numbers.

These are—

$\frac{1}{4}$ = पा *pá*, पाव *páwa.*
$\frac{1}{3}$ = तिहाइ *tehái* or तेहाइ *tĕhái.*
$\frac{1}{2}$ = अद्धा *addhá* or आधा *ádhá.*
$\frac{3}{4}$ = पौन *paun* or पौना *pauná.*
$-\frac{1}{4}$ = पौने *paune.*
$1\frac{1}{4}$ or $+\frac{1}{4}$ = सवा *sawá*, सवाइ *sawái.*
$1\frac{1}{2}$ = डेढ़ *ḍeṛh* or डेढ़ा *ḍeṛhá.*
$2\frac{1}{2}$ = अढ़ाइ *aṛhái.*
$+\frac{1}{2}$ = साढ़े *sáṛhe.*

§ 18. Multiplicatives.

Multiplicatives, such as the English 'twice' and 'thrice,' are not found in this dialect. The Bihárí idiom is illustrated in such phrases as दू सते चौदह *dú sate chaudah*, 'two seven's, fourteen ;' छव तो अठारह *chhaw tí*

* The first three ordinals follow pronominal genitives in the formation of oblique forms. See *post*, § 34.

aṭhárah, 'six three's, eighteen,' which correspond to the English idioms 'seven times two' and 'three times six.' Numbers thus used are called multiplicatives, and differ in some respects from the cardinals. The following are the multiplicative numbers up to 10, including fractions :—

× 1, का *ka.*
× 1¼, सवठ *sawa*, सवैया *sawaiyá*, सवैएँ *sawaiẽ.*
× 1½, डेउढ़ा *ḍĕuṛhá*, डेउढ़े *ḍĕuṛhe.*
× 2, दूना *dúná*, दूनी *dúní.*
× 2½, धाम *dhám*, अढ़ैया *aṛhaiyá*, अढ़ैएँ *aṛhaiẽ.*
× 3, ती *tí*, तिया *tiyá*, तियाँइ *tiyā̃i*, तिरिका *tiriká.*
× 3½, हुँठा *hũṭhá*, हुँठे *hũṭhe.*
× 4, चौका *chauká*, चौके *chauke.*
× 4½, धौँचा *dhaũchá*, धौँचे *dhaũche.*
× 5, पचे *pache*, पञ्जे *pañje.*
× 5½, पहुञ्चा *pahuñchá*, पहुञ्चे *pahuñche.*
× 6, छक *chhak*, छक्का *chhakká*, or छके *chhake.*
× 6½, खौँचा *khaũchá*, खौँचे *khaũche.*
× 7, सते *sate.*
× 8, अट्ठे *áṭṭhe.*
× 9, नवाँ *nawā́*, नवाँइ *nawā̃i.*
× 10, दहाँइ *dahā̃i*, दहैएँ *dahaiẽ.*

§ 19. Definite Cardinals.

These are as follows :—

दूनो *dúno*, दोनो *dono*, 'the two,' 'both ;'
तीनो *tíno*, 'the three ;'
चारो *cháro*, 'the four ;' and so on,

adding ओ *o* to the numerals, after omitting a final short vowel. Example: पाँचो भाइ जौरे हथ *pā̃cho bhái jaure hath*, 'the five brothers are an undivided family.'

§ 20. Indefinite Cardinals.

The termination अन *an* added to the numbers 'one hundred,' 'one thousand,' and so on, always denotes an indefinite number of these aggregates. In this idiom सैकर *saikar* is always substituted for सै *sai*, 'one hundred.' Examples are सैकॱरन पेड़ *saĭk'ran per̤*, 'hundreds of trees;' हजारन *hajáran*, 'thousands;' लाखन *lákhan*, 'tens of thousands;' हजारन अदिमी मरॱलन्ह *hajáran adimí marilanh*, 'thousands of men died.'

§ 21. Collective Numerals.

These—viz. जोड़ा *jor̤á*, 'a pair,' गंडा *gaṇḍá*, 'a four'—are the same as in High Hindí, except सैकॱरा *saĭk'rá*, 'a hundred.'

CHAPTER III.

PRONOUNS.

§ 22. The following tables show the declensional forms of the principal pronouns and pronominal forms.

The declension of pronouns presents some important points of difference from that of nouns, which must be carefully noticed.

While nouns frequently remain unchanged before post-positions, pronouns, with few exceptions, change to some other form, called the *oblique* or *inflected base.*

The accusative singular of pronouns is, with one or two exceptions, never the same as the nominative. The only exception is कुछ *kuchh*, 'anything,' 'something.' In circumstances corresponding to those in which the accusative of a noun takes the nominative form, the accusative of a pronoun takes the oblique form without any post-position.

The genitive forms of pronouns ending in र *r* and न *n* are also to be noticed. They have all oblique forms ending in रा *rá* or ना *ná*, for which see § 34.

Pronouns have the same form, whether referring to masculine or feminine nouns. With the exception of the pronouns of the second person, they all want the vocative case.

§ 23. Pronouns of the First Person and of the Second Person Non-Honorific.

These pronouns have each two forms, a shorter and a longer.

हम *ham*, 'I.'

Singular.

	Shorter form.	*Longer form.*
Nom.	*Wanting.*	हम *ham.*
Acc.	मोरा [1] *morá* or मोरा के *morá ke.*	हमरा [1] *ham'rá* or हमरा के *ham'rá ke.*
Instr.	मोरा से *morá se.*	हमरा से *ham'rá se.*
Dat.	मोरा के *morá ke.*	हमरा के *ham'rá ke.*
Abl.	मोरा से *morá se.*	हमरा से *ham'rá se.*
Gen.	मोर *mor.*	हम्मर *hammar,* हमर *hamar.*
Loc.	मोरा में *morá mẽ.*	हमरा में *ham'rá mẽ.*
Voc.	*Wanting.*	*Wanting.*

[1] मोरो *moro* and हमरो *ham'ro* may be used for मोरा *morá* and हमरा *ham'rá* in an emphatic sense : thus हमरो द *ham'ro da,* 'give to me also.'

Plural.

	Shorter form.	*Longer form.*
Nom.	हमनी [1] *hamaní.*	हमरा सभ [2] *ham'rá sabh.*
Acc.	हमनी (के) *hamaní* (*ke*).	हमरा सभ (के) *ham'rá sabh* (*ke*).
Instr.	हमनी से *hamaní se.*	हमरा सभ से *ham'rá sabh se.*
Dat.	हमनी के *hamaní ke.*	हमरा सभ के *ham'rá sabh ke.*
Abl.	हमनी से *hamaní se.*	हमरा सभ से *ham'rá sabh se.*
Gen.	हमनी कै *hamaní kĕ.*	हमरा सभ कै *ham'rá sabh kĕ.*
Loc.	हमनी में *hamaní mẽ.*	हमरा सभ में *ham'rá sabh mẽ.*
Voc.	*Wanting.*	*Wanting.*

[1] Or हम सभ *ham'sabh,* and so throughout.

[2] In Western Muzaffarpúr a Bhojpúrí nominative plural हमरहिनका *hamar'hin'ká* and oblique plural हमरहिन *hamar'hin* are also used.

तों *tō* or तूं *tū*, 'thou.'

Singular.

	Shorter form.	*Longer form.*
Nom.	तों or तूं *tō* or *tū*.	तों or तूं *tō* or *tū*.
Acc.	तोरा,[1] तोरा के *torá* or *torá ke*.	तोह्‌रा[1] or तोह्‌रा के *tŏh'rá* or *tŏh'rá ke*
Instr.	तोरा से *torá se*.	तोह्‌रा से *tŏh'rá se*.
Dat.	तोरा के *torá ke*.	तोह्‌रा के *tŏh'rá ke*.
Abl.	तोरा से *torá se*.	तोह्‌रा से *tŏh'rá se*.
Gen.	तोर *tor*.	तोहर *tohar*.
Loc.	तोरा में *torá mē*.	तोह्‌रा में *tŏh'rá mē*.
Voc.	हे तों *he tō* or हे तूं *he tū*.	हे तों *he tō* or हे तूं *he tū*.

[1] तोरो *toro* and तोह्‌रो *tŏh'ro* may be used for तोरा *torá* and तोह्‌रा *tŏh'rá* in an emphatic sense: thus तोह्‌रो देखैछी *tŏh'ro dĕkhaichhí*, 'I see you also.'

Plural.

	Shorter form.	*Longer form.*
Nom.	तोहनी[1] *tŏhani*.	तोह्‌रा सभ[2] *tŏh'rá sabh*.
Acc.	तोहनी (के) *tŏhani (ke)*.	तोह्‌रा सभ (के) *tŏh'rá sabh (ke)*.
Instr.	तोहनी से *tŏhani se*.	तोह्‌रा सभ से *tŏhrá sabh se*.
Dat.	तोहनी के *tŏhani ke*.	तोह्‌रा सभ के *tŏh'rá sabh ke*.
Abl.	तोहनी से *tŏhani sē*.	तोह्‌रा सभ से *tŏh'rá sabh se*.
Gen.	तोहनी के *tŏhaní kĕ*.	तोह्‌रा सभ के *tŏh'rá sabh kĕ*.
Loc.	तोहनी में *tŏhani mē*.	तोह्‌रा सभ में *tŏh'rá sabh mē*.
Voc.	हे तूं सभ *he tū sabh*.	हे तूं सभ *he tū sabh*.

[1] Or तों सभ *tō sabh*, and so throughout.

[2] In Western Muzaffarpúr a Bhojpúrí nominative plural तोहर्‌हिन्‌का *tŏhar'hin'ká* and oblique plural तोहर्‌हिन *tŏhar'hin*, are also used.

§ 24. Pronoun of the Second Person Honorific and Reflexive Pronoun.

आहाँ *áhã́* or अपन्ने *ap'nĕ*, 'your honor.

This pronoun is declined regularly like a substantive: thus—

> आहाँ के *áhã́ ke* or अपन्ने के *ap'nĕ ke.*
> आहाँ से *áhã́ se* or अपन्ने से *ap'nĕ se, &c.*

The nominative plural is आहाँ सभ *áhã́ sabh* or अपन्ने सभ *ap'nĕ sabh.* In Western Muzaffarpúr the Bhojpúrí form रउरा *raüra* or रौरा *raurá*, 'your honor,' is also used. It is also declined regularly except in its genitive singular, which is राउर *ráur*.

अपन्ने *ap'ne*, 'self.'

Nominative singular अपन्ने *ap'nĕ*: accusative अपन्ने के *ap'nĕ ke* or अपन्ना के *ap'ná ke*: instrumental अपन्ने से *ap'nĕ se* or अपन्ना से *ap'ná se*, and so on. Genitive singular अप्पन *appan*, अपन *apan*, or आपन *ápan*.

Nominative plural अपन्ने सभ *ap'nĕ sabh*, अपन्ना सभ *ap'ná sabh*, or अप्पन सभ *appan sabh*. The rest is regular.

§ 25. Demonstrative Pronouns.

There are (1) the proximate demonstrative ई *í*, 'this,' and (2) the remote demonstrative ऊ *ú*, 'that.'

Like the personal pronouns, they have each two forms, a shorter and a longer.

ई *í*, 'this.'

Singular.

	Shorter form.	*Longer form.*
Nom.	ई *í*.	ई *í*.
Acc.	एह[1] (के) *ĕh*[1] (*ke*).	एकरा (के) *ĕk'rá* (*ke*).
Instr.	एह से *ĕh se*.	एकरा से *ĕk'rá se*.
Dat.	एह के *ĕh ke*.	एकरा के *ĕk'rá ke*.
Abl.	एह से *ĕh se*.	एकरा से *ĕk'rá se*.
Gen.	एह के *ĕh kĕ*.	एकर *ekar*.
Loc.	एह मेँ, *ĕh mẽ*.	एकरा मेँ *ĕk'rá mẽ*.

[1] एहि *ĕhi*, ए *e*, or एई *ĕí* may be substituted for एह *ĕh* throughout.

Plural.

	Shorter form.	*Longer form.*
Nom.	ई सभ *í sabh*.	ई सभ *í sabh*.
Acc.	इन्ह[1] (के) *inh* (*ke*).	इन्हकरा[2] (के) *inh'kará* (*ke*).
Instr.	इन्ह से *inh se*.	इन्हकरा से *inh'kará se*.
Dat.	इन्ह के *inh ke*.	इन्हकरा के *inh'kará ke*.
Abl.	इन्ह से *inh se*.	इन्हकरा से *inh'kará se*.
Gen.	इन्ह के *inh kĕ*.	इन्हकर *inh'kar*.
Loc.	इन्ह मेँ *inh mẽ*.	इन्हकरा मेँ, *inh'kará mẽ*.

[1] Or हिन्ह *hinh*, इन *in*, or हिन *hin*, and so throughout.

[2] Or हिन्हकरा *hinh'kará*, इन्हका *inh'ká*, हिन्हका *hinh'ká*, इनकरा *in'kará*, हिनकरा *hin'kará*, इनका *in'ká*, or हिनका *hin'ká*, and so throughout.

NOTE.—The plural of this pronoun is used in a singular honorific sense. To form the non-honorific plural, the word सभ *sabh* is added to any of the above forms: thus, nominative plural ई सभ *í sabh*, एकरा सभ *ĕk'rá sabh*, इन्ह सभ *inh sabh*, हिन्हकरा सभ *hinh'kará sabh*, and so on.

ऊ *ú*, 'that.'

The close analogy between the declension of this pronoun and that of ई *í*, 'this,' will be manifest from the following paradigm:—

Singular.

	Shorter form.	*Longer form.*
Nom.	ऊ *ú*.	ऊ *ú*.
Acc.	ओह[1] (के) *ŏh*[1] (*ke*).	ओकरा (के) *ŏk'rá* (*ke*).
Instr.	ओह से *ŏh se*.	ओकरा से *ŏk'rá se*.
Dat.	ओह के *ŏh ke*.	ओकरा के *ŏk'rá ke*.
Abl.	ओह से *ŏh se*.	ओकरा से *ŏk'rá se*.
Gen.	ओह के *ŏh kĕ*.	ओकर *okar*.
Loc.	ओह में *ŏh mẽ*.	ओकरा में *ŏk'rá mẽ*.

[1] ओहि *ŏhi*, ओ *o*, or ओइ *ŏí* may be substituted for ओह *ŏh* throughout.

Plural.

	Shorter form.	*Longer form.*
Nom.	ऊ सभ *ú sabh*.	ऊ सभ *ú sabh*.
Acc.	उन्ह[1] (के) *unh* (*ke*).	उन्हकरा[2] (के) *unh'kará* (*ke*).
Instr.	उन्ह से *unh se*.	उन्हकरा से *unh'kará se*.
Dat.	उन्ह के *unh ke*.	उन्हकरा के *unh'kará ke*.
Abl.	उन्ह से *unh se*.	उन्हकरा से *unh'kará se*.
Gen.	उन्ह के *unh kĕ*.	उन्हकर *unh'kar*.
Loc.	उन्ह में *unh mẽ*.	उन्हकरा में *unh'kará mẽ*.

[1] Or हुन्ह *hunh*, उन *un*, or हुन *hun*, and so throughout.

[2] Or हुन्हकरा *hunh'kará*, उन्हका *unh'ká*, हुन्हका *hunh'ká*, उनकरा *un'kará*, हुनकरा *hun'kará*, उनका *un'ká*, or हुनका *hun'ká*, and so throughout.

NOTE.—The plural of this pronoun is used in a singular honorific sense. To form the non-honorific plural, the word सभ *sabh* is added to any of the above forms: thus, nominative plural ऊ सभ *ú sabh*, ओकरा सभ *ŏk'rá sabh*, उन्ह सभ *unh sabh*, हुन्हकरा सभ *hunh'kará sabh*, and so on.

NOTE.—In the above two demonstrative pronouns the shorter form may be used either adjectivally or substantivally, but the longer form can only be used as a substantive, and never as an adjective.

§ 26. Correlative Pronouns.

These are (1) the relative pronoun जे *je*, 'who;' (2) the correlative pronoun से *se*, 'that;' and (3) the interrogative pronoun के *ke*, 'who?'

The close analogy between their forms should be noted. Like the personal and demonstrative pronouns, they have each a shorter and a longer form.

It is not necessary to give their declension in full, as it is on exactly the same lines as that of the demonstrative pronouns. I shall therefore give only the nominative, genitive, and general oblique forms for each number.

Relative.

जे *je*, 'who.'

Singular.

	Shorter form.	*Longer form.*
Nom.	जे *je* or जौन *jaun*.	*Wanting*.
Gen.	जेह के *jĕh kĕ*.	जेकर *jekar*.
Obl.	जेह, *jĕh*.	जेकरा *jĕk'rá*.

Plural.

Nom.	जे सभ *je sabh*.	जे सभ *je sabh*.
Gen.	जिन्ह के *jinh kĕ*.	जिन्हकर *jinh'kar*.
Obl.	जिन्ह *jinh*.	जिन्हकरा *jinh'kará*.

Correlative.

से *se*, 'that.'

Singular.

	Shorter form.	*Longer form.*
Nom.	से *se*, ते *te*, or तौन *taun*.	*Wanting*.
Gen.	तेह के *tĕh kĕ*.	तेकर *tekar*.
Obl.	तेह *tĕh*.	तेकरा *tĕk'rá*.

Plural.

Nom.	से सभ *se sabh*.	से सभ *se sabh*.
Gen.	तिन्ह के *tinh kĕ*.	तिन्हकर *tinh'kar*.
Obl.	तिन्ह *tinh*.	तिन्हकरा *tinh'kará*.

Interrogative.

के *ke*, 'who?'

Singular.

	Shorter form.	*Longer form.*
Nom.	के *ke* or कौन *kaun.*	*Wanting.*
Gen.	केह के *kĕh kĕ.*	केकर *kekar.*
Obl.	केह *kĕh.*	केकऽरा *kĕk'rá.*

Plural.

Nom.	के सभ *ke sabh.*	के सभ *ke sabh.*
Gen.	किन्ह के *kinh kĕ.*	किन्हऽकर *kinh'kar.*
Obl.	किन्ह *kinh.*	किन्हऽकरा *kinh'kará.*

Other optional forms as in the demonstrative pronouns.

NOTE.—In the above correlative pronouns the shorter form may be used either adjectivally or substantivally, but the longer form can only be used as a substantive, and never as an adjective. As in the case of the demonstrative pronouns, the non-honorific plural is formed by adding सभ *sabh.*

§ 27. Interrogative Pronoun.

SUBSTANTIVAL.

का *ká* or की *kí*, 'what?'

This pronoun is really a neuter form of के *ke,* and can only refer to inanimate things. Its plural is the same as that of के *ke.*

Singular.

Nom. का *ká,* की *kí,* कथी *kathí,* or केथी *kĕthí.*
Obl. कथी *kathí,* केथी *kĕthí,* or काहे *káhĕ.*

Declined regularly like a substantive. Its dative,—केथी ला *kĕthí lá* or कथी ला *kathí lá,* 'for that,' is used as an adverb, meaning 'why.'

§ 28. Indefinite Pronoun.

केऊ *kĕú*, 'anyone,' 'some one.'

When used as an adjective, this pronoun takes also the form कौनो *kaunŏ* or कउनो *kaünŏ*.

Nom. केऊ *kĕú*, or केहू *kĕhú*, or कौनो *kaunŏ*.

Obl. केकऽरो *kĕk'rŏ*, केथियो *kĕthiyŏ*, केऊ *kĕú*, or केहू *kĕhú*.

Declined regularly like a substantive, except the genitive, which is केकऽरो *kĕk'rŏ* only.

PLURAL.—Wanting.

§ 29. The indefinite pronoun कुछ *kuchh*, कुछु *kuchhu*, कुछुओ *kuchhuŏ*, किछु *kichhu*, or किछिओ *kichhiŏ*, and तनिक *tanik* or कनिक *kanik*, 'anything,' 'something,' is declined regularly like a substantive: thus कुछु के *kuchhu ke*, कुछु से *kuchhu se*, &c.

§ 30. The indefinite pronoun सभ *sabh*, 'all,' 'every one,' is declined regularly like a substantive. When plurality is to be emphasised, it has an oblique plural form सभन *sabhan*: thus, सभ के *sabh kĕ*, 'of all,' *taken as a whole*; but सभन के *sabhan kĕ*, 'of all,' *taken severally*.

§ 31. The indefinite pronouns जेकेऊ *jekĕú*, 'whoever,' and जेकुछु *jekuchhu*, 'whatever,' are compounds, and are declined regularly like their component parts: thus, acc. sing. जेह केकऽरो *jĕh kĕk'rŏ*, जेह कुछु *jĕh kuchhu*; instr. जेह केकऽरो से *jĕh kĕk'rŏ se*, &c.

The indefinite pronominal adjective कै *kai*, कइ *kaï*, or कइक *kaïk* signifies 'several.' It is also used as an interrogative, meaning 'how many?'

§ 32. Derivative Pronominal Forms.

The following table gives the more usual pronominal adjectives and adverbs in a succinct form.

		Pronoun.	Manner.	
			Pron. Adj.	Pron. Adv.
Demonstrative ...	Proximate ...	ई *í*, 'this' ...	ऐसन *aisan*, 'of this kind.'	ऐसे *aise*, 'thus.'
	Remote ...	ऊ *ú*, 'that' ...	वैसन *waisan*, 'of that kind.'	वैसे *waise*, 'in that way.'
Relative		जे *je*, 'who' ...	जैसन *jaisan*, 'of what kind.'	जैसे *jaise*, 'in what way.'
Correlative		से *se*, 'that' ...	तैसन *taisan*, 'of that kind.'	तैसे *taise*, 'in that way.'
Interrogative		के *ke*, 'who?' ...	कैसन *kaisan*, 'of what kind?'	कैसे *kaise*, 'in what way?'

Pron. adj. of Quantity.	Pron. adv. of Time.	Pron. adv. of Place.	Pron. adv. of Direction.
एतेक *ĕtĕk*, एतऽना *ĕt'ná*, 'this much.'	एहिया *ĕhiyá*, 'now.'	इहाँ *ihā́*, 'here.'	एन्ने *ĕnnĕ*, हेन्ने *hĕnnĕ*, or एम्हर *emhar*, 'hither.'
ओतेक *ŏtĕk*, ओतऽना *ŏt'ná*, 'that much.'	ओहिया *ŏhiyá*, 'then.'	उहाँ *uhā́*, 'there.'	ओन्ने *ŏnnĕ*, ओम्हर *omhar*, 'thither.'
जेतेक *jĕtĕk*, जेतऽना *jĕt'ná*, 'how much.'	जहिया *jahiyá*, 'when.'	जहाँ *jahā́*, 'where.'	जेन्ने *jĕnnĕ*, जेम्हर *jemhar*, 'whither.'
तेतेक *tĕtĕk*, तेतऽना *tĕt'ná*, 'so much.'	तहिया *tahiyá*, 'then.'	तहाँ *tahā́*, 'there.'	तेन्ने *tĕnnĕ*, तेम्हर *temhar*, 'thither.'
केतेक *kĕtĕk*, केतऽना *kĕt'ná*, 'how much?'	कहिया *kahiyá*, 'when?'	कहाँ *kahā́*, 'where?'	केन्ने *kĕnnĕ*, केम्हर *kemhar*, 'whither?'

§ 33. Adjectival Pronouns.

The following sentences are designed to show the use of the various pronouns, both adjectivally and substantivally. Before doing so it is best to note here that colloquially the oblique forms एह *ĕh*, ओह *ŏh*, जेह *jĕh*, तेह *tĕh*, and केह *kĕh*, are frequently written and pronounced ए *e*, ओ *o*, जे *je*, ते *te*, and के *ke* respectively.

NOTE that while जे *je*, जौन *jaun*, से *se*, तौन *taun*, are used either as adjectives or substantives in both the nominative and oblique cases, के *ke* can only be used as an adjective in the nominative case. In the oblique cases, when used as an adjective, के *ke* always becomes कौन *kaun* or कौना *kauná* (also, of course, spelt कउन *kaün* or कउना *kaüná*). Moreover, when used in the *oblique* cases as adjectives, जौन *jaun* (or जउन *jaün*) and तौन *taun* (or तउन *taün*) may optionally become जौना *jauná* (or जउना *jaüná*) and तौना *tauná* (or तउना *taüná*) respectively.

The examples are in the dialect of Eastern Muzaffarpúr.

(1) जे आएल रहे, से गेल, *je áĕl rahe, se gel:* 'he who had come, went.'

(2) जे लोग आएल रहे, से लोग गेल, *je log áĕl rahe, se log gel:* 'the man who had come, went.'

(3) जेकर खेत, तेकर धान, *jekar khet, tekar dhán:* 'he who owns the field, owns the paddy.'

(4) जे (or जौन or जौना) लोग के खेत, ते (or तौन or तौना) लोग के धान *je* (or *jaun* or *jauná*) *log kĕ khet, te* (or *taun* or *tauná*) *log kĕ dhán:* 'the man who owns the field, owns the paddy.'

(5) के रहे *ke rahe?* 'who was it?'

(6) ऊ के (or कौन) लोग हथ *ú ke* (or *kaun*) *log hath?* 'what caste is he?'

(7) केकर घोड़ा है *kekar ghoṛá hai?* 'whose is the horse?'

(8) की है *kí hai?* 'what is it?'

(9) कौन बिरिछ है, *kaun birichh hai?* 'what tree is it?'

(10) कथी में पानि लैलह ह *kathí mẽ páni laila ha?* 'in what have you brought the water?'

(11) कौना लोटा में पानि लैलह ह *kauná loṭá mẽ páni laila ha?* 'in what *loṭa* have you brought the water?'

(12) कौनो न॰ आएल *kaunŏ na áĕl*, 'no one came.'

(13) केहू लरिका न॰ आएल *kĕhú lariká na áĕl*, 'no boy came.'

(14) ऊ गाँव मेँ केक॰रो किछु न॰ है *ú gāw mē kĕk'rŏ kichhu na hai*, 'in that village no one has anything.'

(15) ऊ गाँव के केहू बनियाँ से किछु न॰ मिल॰तै *ú gāw kĕ kĕhú baniyā se kichhu na mil'tai*, 'in that village nothing will be got from any shopkeeper.'

(16) ऊ दवाइ के केथियो मेँ धरे के* होअत *ú dawāi ke kĕthiyŏ mĕ dharĕ ke* hoăt*, 'it will be (necessary) to put that medicine into something.'

(17) कै अदिमी ऐलन्ह *kai adimí ailanh*, 'several men came,' or 'how many men came?'

§ 34. The Pronominal Oblique Genitive.

The following are examples of pronominal genitives which end in र *r* or न *n*, and which have an oblique form ending in रा *rá* or ना *ná*. These oblique forms occur for all pronominal genitives ending in र *r*, and are used with nouns in any form except that of the nominative singular or plural:—

Direct Genitive.	Meaning.	Oblique form.
मोर *mor*.	'My.'	मोरा *morá*.
हम्मर *hammar*.	'My.'	हम॰रा *ham'rá*.
तोर *tor*.	'Thy.'	तोरा *torá*.
तोहर *tohar*.	'Thy.'	तोह॰रा *tŏh'rá*.
अप्पन *appan*.	'Own.'	अप॰ना *ap'ná*.
एकर *ekar*.	'Of this.'	एक॰रा *ĕk'rá*.
ओकर *okar*.	'Of that,' 'his.'	ओक॰रा *ŏk'rá*.
जेकर *jekar*.	'Whose.'	जेक॰रा *jĕk'rá*.
तेकर *tekar*.	'His.'	तेक॰रा *tĕk'rá*.
केकर *kekar*.	'Whose?'	केक॰रा *kĕk'rá*.

* Dative of the verbal noun.

The following examples will show the use of the génitive in—(*a*) its direct form, (*b*) its oblique form.

a.—Genitives agreeing with nouns in the nominative form, *i.e.* direct genitives.

ओकर मौगी कैसन सुन्दर है *okar maugi kaisan sundar hai*, 'how beautiful his wife is!'

केकर बेटा है *kekar beṭá hai ?* 'whose son is he?'

हम्मर धंधा बिगरत्तै *hammar dhandhá bigar'tai*, 'my profession will be ruined.'

ओकर कानल सुन के *okar kánal sun kĕ*, 'on hearing her lamentations.'

ओकर इकरार लिखऽ *okar ik'rár likha*, 'write a bond to that effect' (*lit.* of that).

अप्पन सभ धन उड़ा पड़ा कऽ, भिखार हो गेल *appan sabh dhan uṛá paṛá ka, bhikhár ho gel*, 'having wasted all his substance, he became poor.'

b.—Genitives agreeing with nouns not in the nominative form, *i.e.* oblique genitives.

ओकरा चढ़े के घोड़ा *ŏk'rá chaṛhĕ kĕ ghoṛá*, his riding-horse' (*lit.* the horse of his riding.)

ऊ ओकरा फुलवारी मेँ आएल *ú ŏk'rá phul'wárí mẽ áĕl*, 'he came into *his* (some one else's) garden.'

हमरा सिरकी मेँ *ham'rá sir'kí mẽ*, 'in my hovel.'

तोहरा घर मेँ *tŏh'rá ghar mẽ*, 'in your house.'

तोहरा हथवा से *tŏh'rá hath'wá se*, 'from thy hand.'

हमरा दरवाजा से ओकर दरवाजा बाँस भर अलग है *ham'rá dar'wájá se okar dar'wájá bā̃s bhar alag hai*, 'his doorway is a rod, distance from mine.'

गिरहस्त अपना जी मेँ कहलक *gir'hast ap'ná ji mẽ kah'lak*, 'the husbandman said in his heart.'

Sometimes, by the vulgar, the direct form is used instead of the oblique, but the oblique form is never used instead of the direct.

DIVISION II.

CONJUGATION.

CHAPTER IV.

INTRODUCTORY.

§ 35. It must be noted with respect to the following paradigms that colloquially the plural is commonly used in the place of the singular: thus तोँ हऽ *tō ha*, 'thou art,' is commonly used instead of तोँ हए *tō hae*, which is the more correct form. It is important to note this. Distinction of number is only found in poetry. In common talk the singular is commonly used in a non-honorific, and the plural in an honorific sense, exactly like Uriyá or Bangálí.

Note also that there is great laxity colloquially in regard to gender. The forms given for the feminine are only those which are specially confined to that gender; but instead of these, the masculine forms are often used colloquially. In the following paradigms when the masculine and feminine forms coincide, the latter are not given. As a matter of fact feminine forms are rarely used except in the west of the district. Perhaps the second plural feminine is the one which is most current.

§ 35*a*. As already observed (§ 1), the language spoken in Central and South Muzaffarpúr is in the main Maithilí. In the western part of the district, however, many Bhojpúrí forms are used, and such will be noted in their proper places.

Besides the personal forms given, each tense has a special honorific form common to the second and third persons, which will, in the case of the radical and participial tenses, be duly noted. It has not been thought necessary to do so in the case of the periphrastic tenses.

§ 36. With regard to the spelling of the various tense-forms, it must be noted that ऐ *ai* and औ *au* are frequently written अइ *aï* and अउ *aü* respectively: thus such forms as गिर॰लै *gir'lai* and गिर॰लौ *gir'lau* are often written गिर॰लइ *gir'laï* and गिर॰लउ *gir'laü*. It has not been thought-necessary to put both these varieties of spelling into the paradigms: hence only गिर॰लै *gir'lai*, गिर॰लौ *gir'lau*, *&c.*, will be found therein. With regard to this and to the shortening of antepenultimate vowels, see General Introduction, §§ 34—37.

It must be noted that a great many verbal forms have a heavy diphthong, viz. ऐ *ai* or औ *au*, in the last syllable. When this occurs in any form (except in the present conjunctive), any preceding long vowel is shortened. Thus we have भॆलैक *bhĕlaik*, 'he became,' दॆखैत *dĕkhait*, 'seeing,' and not भेलैक *bhelaik* or देखैत *dekhait*, as would be required by General Introduction, § 37. In the present conjunctive, however, a preceding vowel remains long, so that we have देखै *dekhai*, '(if) he sees,' and not दॆखै *dĕkhai*.

NOTE also that every plural form ending in न्ह *nh* can also be spelt as ending in न *n*: thus गिर॰लन्ह *gir'lanh* or गिर॰लन *gir'lan*. Only the fuller form in न्ह *nh* will be given in the paradigms.

§ 37. Conjugational System.

The conjugation of the verb √ देख *dekh*, 'see,' being given in full, it is not necessary to give here the details of conjugation at length.

§ 38. There are three moods—the Indicative, Conjunctive, and Imperative. These may again be divided into *simple tenses*—formed from the root direct, and *periphrastic tenses*—formed with the aid of auxiliary verbs added to the present or past participle, or to the conjugated preterite indicative.

§ 39. The *simple tenses* are as follows:—

INDICATIVE.	CONJUNCTIVE.	IMPERATIVE.
Present.	Present.	Present.
Preterite.	Preterite.	
Future.		

Of these, the present imperative is always the same as the present conjunctive.

§ 40. The *periphrastic tenses* are as follows:—

a) From the present participle, direct form—

Indicative—

Definite present	with auxiliary	present.
Imperfect	„	preterite.
Durative future	„	future.

Conjunctive—

Future	with auxiliary	present conjunctive.
Durative present	„	preterite „

b) From the past participle: direct form in the neuter verb, oblique form in the active verb—

Indicative—

Perfect (form II)	with auxiliary	present.
Pluperfect (form II)	„	past.
Future exact	„	future.

Conjunctive—

Future exact	with auxiliary	present conjunctive.
Preterite	„	preterite.

c) From the preterite indicative—

Indicative—

Perfect (form I)	with auxiliary	present.
Pluperfect (form I)	„	preterite.

Concerning the use of the auxiliary in tenses formed from the past participle, see General Introduction, p. 13, cl. (4).

§ 41. The Simple Tenses.

The personal terminations are nearly the same for all these tenses. They are added to a tense-stem, the formation of which will be described afterwards. They are exactly the same for the present conjunctive, the preterite indicative, and the preterite conjunctive.

The terminations of these three tenses are given in the following table. It will be observed that there are many optional forms of terminations for each person. They are all used with nearly equal frequency. They should be carefully committed to memory.

It must be noted that the termination अह *ah* or अ *a* of the 2nd plural masculine is pronounced with a peculiar drawl, something like the English word 'awe.' Thus, देखऽ *dekh*'awe.' So also is pronounced the penultimate अ *a* of the Bhojpúrí present indicative: thus देखलों *dekhalō*, 'I see,' pronounced *dekh*'awe'*lō*; देखलऽ *dekhala*, 'you see,' pronounced *dekh* 'awe'*l*'awe.'

Table showing the Personal Terminations of the Present Conjunctive, the Preterite Indicative, and the Preterite Conjunctive.

Person.	SINGULAR.		PLURAL.	
	Masculine.	Feminine.	Masculine.	Feminine.
1st	आँ *ō*, औं *aũ*.		ईं *ī*, इऐन्ह *iainh*.	
2nd	ए *e*, अस *as*.*	इस *is*.*	अह *ah*, अ *a*, ऽहोक *'hok*.	ऊ *ú*.*
3rd	ए *e*.		अथ *ath*. ऽथिन्ह *'thinh*. ऽथुन्ह *'thunh*. अन्ह *anh*.	इन्ह *inh*.*

* These are Bhojpúrí forms, only used in the west of the district. It will be noticed that they include all the feminine forms. The 2nd plural feminine is, however, used more generally.

§ 42. These terminations are added to various tense-stems, and it is by these tense-stems that the tenses are distinguished. The formation of each tense-stem will be given separately under the heading of each tense, and the conjugation of each tense will now be described in the order in which they will subsequently be given in the conjugation of the model verb √ देख *dekh*, 'see.'

§ 43 (a). The Present Indicative.

This tense is borrowed from Bhojpúrí, and is only used in the west of the district. It is conjugated by adding the following terminations to the root :—

Person.	Singular.		Plural.	
	Masculine.	Feminine.	Masculine.	Feminine.
1st	अलों *alõ.* ऍलों *ĕlõ.*		ईला *ílá*, ईले *íle.* ऐली *aïlí*, अली *alí.*	
2nd	अले *ale.* ऍले *ĕle.*	अलिस *alis.* ऍलिस *ĕlis.*	अलऽ *ala.* ऍलऽ *ĕla.*	
3rd	अला *alá.* ऍला *ĕlá.*		अले *ale*, अलन्ह *alanh.* ऍले *ĕle*, ऍलन्ह *ĕlanh.*	अलिन्ह *alinh.* ऍलिन्ह *ĕlinh.*

Concerning the pronunciation of these terminations, see § 41.

§ 43 (b). The Preterite Indicative.

The stem of this tense is formed by adding अल *al* to the root. To this the terminations in § 41 are added. Thus √ देख *dekh*, 'see,' preterite stem देखल *dekhal*, to which the terminations are added: thus देखलों *dĕkh'lõ*, 'I saw.' This tense has in the case of transitive verbs the following optional terminations:—अक *ăk*, ॰कै *'kai*, ॰कैक *'kaik* for the third person singular, and ॰कैन्ह *'kainh* in the third person plural. In the case of neuter verbs—

(1) in third sing. masc., either no termination is added to the stem at all, or else the following are the terminations,—ए *e*, अक *ak*, ऐ *ai*, ऐक *aik*, औ *au*, or औक *auk*;

(2) in the third plur. masc. in addition to the terminations in § 41, it takes the termination ऐन्ह *ainh*.

Examples.

देख॰ले *dĕkh'le* or देख॰लक *dĕkh'lak*, देखल॰कै *dĕkhal'kai*, देखल॰कैक *dĕkhal'kaik*, 'he saw.' देखल॰कैन्ह *dĕkhal'kainh*, &c., 'they saw.'

गिर॰ले *gir'le* or गिरल *giral*, गिर॰लक *gir'lak*, गिर॰लै *gir'lai*, गिर॰लैक *gir'laik*, गिर॰लौ *gir'lau*, गिर॰लौक *gir'lauk*, 'he fell.' गिर॰लैन्ह *gir'lainh*, &c., 'they fell.'

§ 44. The Future Indicative.

This tense has two stems—one for the first and second persons, and one for the third person. The first stem is formed by adding अब *ab* to the root; the second is the root itself.

The following are the terminations of this tense. All should be added to the root direct.

After certain vowels, *e.g.* आ *á*, the stem terminations may be एब *éb* instead of अब *ab*.

Terminations of the Future.

Person.	SINGULAR.		PLURAL.	
	Masculine.	Feminine.	Masculine.	Feminine.
1st	॰बै *'bai*, ॰बैक *'baik*. ॰बौ *'bau*, ॰बौक *'bauk*.		अब *ab*, ॰बैन्ह *'bainh*.	
2nd	॰बे *'be*.		॰बह *'bah*, ॰बठ *'ba*.	॰बू *bú*.*
3rd	अत, ॰तै, ॰तैक, ॰तौ, ॰तौक *at, 'tai, 'taik, 'tau, 'tauk*, ई *í*.*		॰तन्ह *'tanh*, ॰तैन्ह *'tainh*, इहें *ihĕ*.*	॰तिन्ह *'tinh*.*

* These are Bhojpúrí forms, only used in the west of the district.

§ 45. The Present Conjunctive and Imperative.

In this tense the terminations are added to the root itself: thus देखों *dekhõ*, 'let me see.' As already stated, the terminations are those given in § 41. Besides these, this tense may in the first person singular take the termination ऊ *ú*, and in the third person masculine singular take the following terminations:— ओ *o*, ऐ *ai*, ऐक *aik*, अस *as*. Of these, the last (viz. अस *as*) is Bhojpúrí, and confined to the west of the district. It also optionally takes no termination whatever in the second person singular.

In the third person masculine plural the termination ऐन्ह *ainh* can optionally be used.

§ 46. The Preterite Conjunctive.

In this tense अत *at* or इत *it* is added to the root to form the stem. The personal terminations in § 41 are then added: thus देखःतों *dĕkh'tī*, '(if) I had seen.'

In the third person singular masculine this tense drops the usual terminations and ends in ऐत *ait* or इत *it*, added simply to the root: thus देखैत *dĕkhait* or देखित *dekhit*.

CHAPTER V.

AUXILIARY VERBS.

§ 47. There are two classes of auxiliary verbs, the *defective* and the *complete*.

§ 48. There are five *defective auxiliary verbs*, one from the √अहव *ahw* or हव *haw*, another from the √ अछ *achh*, another from the √ थ *tha*, another from the √ बाट *báṭ*, and another from the √ रह *rah*. They are all more or less irregular in their conjugation.

(*a*) The first is used in the present tense only, and loses its initial vowel. It has two forms, a weak (*e.g.* हऊ *haú*, 'I am,') and a strong (*e.g.* हतू *hatú*, 'I am'). The weak form is very irregular. I shall call it the *first defective auxiliary verb.*

(*b*) The second is used in the present and preterite tenses, and always loses its initial vowel. It has in the present tense two forms, a weak (*e.g.* छौं *chhãũ*, 'I am,') and a strong (*e.g.* छिकौं *chhikõ*, 'I am'). In the preterite tense it is used only in the weak form (*e.g.* छलौं *chhalõ*, 'I was'). I shall call it the *second defective auxiliary verb.*

(*c*) The third is used only in the present tense. It has only one form, the strong (*e.g.* थिकौं *thĭkô*, 'I am'), the weak form not being used. I shall call it the *third defectiue auxiliary verb.*

(*d*) The fourth is borrowed from Bhojpúrí, and is only used in the west of the district. It is used only in the present tense in one form, the weak (*e.g.* बाटौं *báṭõ*, 'I am'). I shall call it the *fourth defective auxiliary verb.*

(*e*) The fifth is used only in the present tense, with, however, a preterite signification. It is hence classified as a preterite. It has only one form, a weak one (*e.g.* रहौ *rahí*, 'I was'). I shall call it the *fifth defective auxiliary verb.*

§ 49. The complete auxiliary verb is formed from the √ हो *ho*, 'become.' It has two forms, a weak (√ हो *ho*) and a strong (√ होख *hokh*), each of wnich is conjugated through all moods and tenses. The first I shall call the *weak complete auxiliary verb*, and the second the *strong complete auxiliary verb*. Its preterite, however, is never used as an auxiliary, but only as a verb substantive.

§ 50. First Defective Auxiliary Verb.

√ अहु *ahw*, √ हव *haw*, 'be,'

Present: '*I am,*' *&c.*

WEAK FORM.

Person.	Singular. Masculine.	Singular. Feminine.	Plural. Masculine.	Plural. Feminine.
1st	हऊ *haú.*		हई *hai*, ही *hí.* हिऐन्ह *hiainh.*	
2nd	हए *haë.* हस *has,** हवस *hawas.**	हिस *his.**	हह *hah*, हठ *ha*, हथठ *hatha.*	हऊ *haú.**
3rd	हठ *ha.* है *hai*, हैक *haik.* हौ *hau*, हौक *hauk.* हवस *hawas.**		हथ *hath*, हथन्ह *hathinh.* हैन्ह *hainh.* हवन्ह *hawanh.*	हविन्ह *hawinh.**

* Bhojpúrí forms peculiar to the west of the district.

Honorific forms for second and third persons: हई *haí* or हथी *hathí.*

STRONG FORM.

Person.	SINGULAR.		PLURAL.	
	Masculine.	Feminine.	Masculine.	Feminine.
1st	हतू hatú.		हती hatí.	
	हतौं hatõ, हतौँ hatãũ.		हतिऐन्ह hatiainh.	
2nd	हत hat, हते hate.		हतह hatah, हतठ hata.	हतू hatú.*
	हतस hatas.*	हतिस hatis.*		
3rd	हते hate, हतो hato.		हतथ hatath, हतःथिन्ह [hat'thinh.	
	हतै hatai, हतैक hataik.		हतैन्ह hatainh.	
	हतस hatas.*		हतन्ह hatanh.	हतिन्ह hatinh.*

* Bhojpúrí forms peculiar to the west of the district.

Honorific forms for second and third persons : हती *hati* or हतौ *hatau*.

§ 51. Second Defective Auxiliary Verb.

√ अछ *achh*, 'be.'

Present : '*I am,*' *&c.*

WEAK FORM.

Person.	SINGULAR.		PLURAL.	
	Masculine.	Feminine.	Masculine.	Feminine.
1st	छौं chhãũ.		छी chhí, छिऐन्ह chhiainh.	
2nd	छे chhe.		छह chhah, छठ chha.	
3rd	छै chhai, छैक chhaik.		छैन्ह chhainh.	
			छथ chhath, छथिन्ह chhathinh.	

Honorific forms for second and third persons : छी *chhi* or छौ *chhau*.

Strong Form.

Person.	Singular. Masculine.	Singular. Feminine.	Plural. Masculine.	Plural. Feminine.
1st	छिकौं, छिकौँ, *chhikō, chhikaũ.*		छिकी, छिकिऐन्ह, *chhiki, chhikiainh.*	
	छतौं, छतौँ, *chhatō, chhataũ.*		छती, छतिऐन्ह, *chhati, chhatiainh.*	
2nd	छिके *chhike.*		छिकह, छिकउ, *chhikah, chhika.*	
	छते *chhate.*		छतह, छतउ, *chhatah, chhata.*	
3rd	छिके *chhike.*		छिकैन्ह *chhikainh.*	
	छिकै *chhikai.*		छिकथ *chhikath.*	
	छिकैक *chhikaik.*		छिकथिन्ह *chhik'thinh.*	
			छतन्ह *chhatanh.*	छतिन्ह *chhatinh.**

* Bhojpúrí form, only used in the west of the district.

Honorific forms for second and third persons : छिकी *chhiki* or छिकौ *chhikau.*

Preterite : '*I was,*' *&c.*

Person.	SINGULAR. Masculine.	SINGULAR. Feminine.	PLURAL. Masculine.	PLURAL. Feminine.
1st	छलों, छलौं, *chhalõ, chhalaũ.*		छली *chhali*, छलिऐन्ह [*chhaliainh.*	
2nd	छले *chhale.*		छलह *chhalah*, छलऽ *chhala*, छल॰होक *chhal'hok.*	छलू *chhalú.**
3rd	छल *chhal*, छलक [*chhalak.*		छलथ, छल॰थिन्ह, *chhalath, chhal'thinh*, छल॰थुन्ह *chhal'thunh.*	
	छले *chhale.*		छलैन्ह *chhalainh.*	
	छलै *chhalai*, छलैक [*chhalaik.*		छलन्ह *chhalanh.*	छलिन्ह *chhalinh.**

* Bhojpúrí forms, only used in the west of the district.

Honorific forms for second and third persons : छलौ *chhali* or छलौ *chhalau.*

§ 52. Third Defective Auxiliary Verb.

√ थ *tha*, 'be.'

Present: '*I am*,' *&c.*

Person.	Singular.		Plural.	
	Masculine.	Feminine.	Masculine.	Feminine.
1st	थिकौं, थिकौँ, *thikõ*, *thikaũ*.		थिकी *thikí*, थिकिऐन्ह [*thikiainh*.	
2nd	थिके *thike*.		थिकह *thikah*, थिकऽ *thika*.	
3rd	थिके *thike*. थिकै, थिकैक, *thikai*, *thikaik*.		थिकथ, थिकथिन्ह, *thikath*, *thik'thinh*, थिकैन्ह *thikainh*.	

Honorific form for second and third persons: थिकी *thikí* or थिकौ *thikau*.

This verb contains no Bhojpúrí forms, and is only used in the east of the district.

§ 52a. Fourth Defective Auxiliary Verb.

√ बाट *báṭ*, 'be.'

Present: '*I am*,' *&c.*

Person.	Singular.		Plural.	
	Masculine.	Feminine.	Masculine.	Feminine.
1st	बाटौं *báṭõ*.		बाटी *báṭí*.	
2nd	बाटे *báṭe*, बाटस *báṭas*.	बाटिस *báṭis*.	बाटह *báṭah*, बाटऽ *báṭah*.	बाटू *báṭú*.
3rd	बाटे *báṭe*, बाटो *báṭo*, बाटै *báṭai*, बाटस *báṭas*, बा *bá*.	बटसि *baṭasi*.	बाटन *báṭan*.	बाटिन *báṭin*.

This verb is borrowed from Bhojpúrí, and is used only in the west of the district.

§ 52b. Fifth Defective Auxiliary Verb.

√ रह *rah*, 'remain.'

Present, *used as a* Preterite: '*I was,*' *&c.*

Person.	SINGULAR.		PLURAL.	
	Masculine.	Feminine.	Masculine.	Feminine.
1st	*Not used.*		रही *rahi.*	
2nd	रहे *rahe.*		रहह *rahah*, रहअ *raha.*	रहू *rahú.**
3rd	रहे *rahe.* रहै *rahai*, रहैक *rahaik.*		रहथ *rahath*, रहन्थिन्ह *rah'thinh.* रहैन्ह *rahainh.*	

* A Bhojpúrí form, only used in the west of the district.

Honorific forms for second and third persons: रही *rahi* or रहौ *rahau.*

§ 53a.—The Weak Complete Auxiliary Verb.

√ हो *ho*, '*be*,' '*become*.'

INDICATIVE MOOD.

(*a*)—Present :* '*I am*,' *&c.*

Person.	Singular.		Plural.	
	Masculine.	Feminine.	Masculine.	Feminine.
1st	होअलों, होएलों, *hoalō*, *hoĕlō*.		होइला, होइले, *hoílá*, *hoíle*.	
2nd	होअले *hoale*, होएले [*hoĕle*.	होअलिस *hoalis*. होएलिस *hoĕlis*.	होअलऽ, होएलऽ, *hoala*, *hoela*.	
3rd	होअला, होएला, *hoalá*, *hoĕlá*.		होअले, होएले, *hoale*, *hoĕle*,	
			होअलन्ह *hoälanh*, होएलन्ह, *hoĕlanh*.	होअलिन्ह *hoalinh*. होएलिन्ह *hoĕlinh*.

* This tense is borrowed from Bhojpúrí, and is only used in the west of the district.

Honorific form for second and third persons : होइले *hoíle*

53b. (*b*)—Preterite: '*I became,*' *&c.*

NOTE.—This tense is never used as an auxiliary, छलौं *chhalõ* or रही *rahí* (see above) being used instead.

Person.	Singular.		Plural.	
	Masculine.	Feminine.	Masculine.	Feminine.
1st	भेलौं *bhelõ*. भेलौँ *bhĕlaũ*.		भेली *bhelí*. भेलिऐन्ह *bhĕliainh*.	
2nd	भेले *bhele*, भेलस *bhelas*.*	भेलिस *bhelis*.*	भेलह *bhelah*, भेलठ *bhela*.	भेलू *bhelú*.*
3rd	भेल *bhel*, भेलक *bhelak*. भेले *bhele*. भेलै *bhĕlai*, भेलैक [*bhĕlaik*. भेलौ *bhĕlau*, भेलौक [*bhĕlauk*.		भेलथ, भेल॰थिन्ह, भेल॰थुन्ह, *bhelath*, *bhĕl'thinh*, *bhel'*- [*thunh*. भेलैन्ह *bhĕlainh*. भेलन्ह *bhelanh*.	भेलिन्ह *bhelinh*.*

* Bhojpúrí forms, only used in the west of the district.

Honorific forms for second and third persons:- भेली *bhelí*, भेलौ *bhĕlau*.

§ 54. (c)—Future : '*I shall be,*' &c.

Person.	Singular.		Plural.	
	Masculine.	Feminine.	Masculine.	Feminine.
1st	होएबै *hŏĕbai*, होएबैक		होएब *hoĕb*, होएबैन्ह *hŏĕ-*	
	[*hŏĕbaik.*		[*bainh.*	
	होएबौ *hŏĕbau*, होएबौक			
	[*hŏĕbauk.*			
2nd	होएबे *hoĕbe.*		होएबह *hoĕbah*, होएबऽ	होएबू *hoĕbú.**
			hoĕba.	
3rd	होअत *hoät.*			
	होतै *hŏtai*,† होतैक			
	[*hŏtaik.*†			
	हतौ *hŏtau*,† होतौक		होतन्ह *hotanh*,† होतैन्ह	होतिन्ह *hotinh.**†
	[*hŏtauk*†.		[*hŏtainh.*†	
	होइ *hot.**		होइहें *hoïhẽ.**	

* Bhojpúrí forms, only used in the west of the district.

† Or होअतै *hŏatai*, होय्‌तै *hŏy'tai*, &c.

Honorific forms for second and third persons : होएब *hoĕb* or होएबैन्ह *hŏebainh.*

CONJUNCTIVE MOOD.

§ 55. (*d*)—Present: '*(If) I be*,' *&c.*

Person.	Singular.		Plural.	
	Masculine.	Feminine.	Masculine.	Feminine.
1st	होऊ *hoú*.		होई *hoí*, होइऐन्ह *hŏiainh*.	
2nd	होए *hoe*. होअस *hoas*.*	होइस *hoïs*.*	होअह *hoah*, होअ *hoa*.	होऊ *hoú*.*
3rd	होए *hoe*. होऐ, होऐक, *hoai*, *hoaik*. होअस *hoas*.*		होअथ. होअथिन्ह, *hoath*, *hoathinh*. होऐन्ह *hoainh*. होअन्ह *hoanh*.	होइन्ह *hoïnh*.*

* Bhojpúrí forms, only used in the west of the district.

Honorific form for second and third persons: होई *hoí*.

§ 56. (*e*)—Preterite: *'(If) I had been,' &c.*

Person.	Singular.		Plural.	
	Masculine.	Feminine.	Masculine.	Feminine.
1st	होइतों *hoïtõ.* होइतौं *hŏïtaũ.*		होइती *hoití.* होइतिऐन्ह *hŏïtiaïnh.*	
2nd	होइते *hoïte.* होइतस *hoïtas.**	होइतिस *hoïtis.**	होइतह *hoïtah*, होइतऽ, [*hoïta.*	होइतू *hoïtú.**
3rd	होइत *hoït.* होऐत *hŏait.*		होइतथ *hoïtath.* होइत॰थिन्ह *hoït'thinh.* होइतन्ह *hoïtanh.*	होइतिन्ह *hoïtinh.**

* Bhojpúrí forms, only used in the west of the district.

Honorific forms for second and third persons: होइती *hoïti* or होइतौ *hŏitau.*

§ 57.—Imperative Mood.

Present: '*Let me see,*' *&c.*

The same as the present conjunctive.

Precative Forms.

Non-honorific—

होइहठ *hoïha.*

Honorific—

होऊ *hoú*, होएब *hoëb*, होइहैं *hoihẽ*, 'be good enough to be.'

The periphrastic tenses are quite regular, and need not be given.

§ 58a. Present Participle, '*being.*'

Singular and Plural.

होइत *hoït* or होऐत *hŏait.*

Past Participle, '*been.*'

भेल *bhel.*

Conjunctive Participle, '*having been.*'

भै कै *bhai kĕ.*

Infinitive, '*to be.*'

होएब *hoĕb.*

§ 58b. The Strong Complete Auxiliary Verb.

√ होख *hokh*, 'be,' 'become.'

This verb is conjugated regularly throughout, exactly like the verb √ देख *dekh*, 'see,' except that, being intransitive, its third person singular preterite is होखल *hokhal*, *&c.*, like गिरल *giral*, *&c.* Its conjugation is therefore not given here.

CHAPTER VI.

THE REGULAR ACTIVE VERB.

§ 59. There is only one conjugation of active verbs, if we except a few irregular verbs to be noted further on. The conjugation of neuter verbs differs from that of active verbs only in certain of the past tenses, and these will be treated of in a future page. Verbs whose roots end in vowels also exhibit slight variations, which will be explained at the proper place. For the sake of uniformity the tenses are given in the same order, and under the same names, as those in Dr. Hœrnle's Grammar.

Reference is again made to General Introduction, §§ 34 to 36, with regard to the changes of the root-vowel.

§ 60. √ देख *dekh*, 'see.'

INFINITIVE: देखल *dekhal.*

PRESENT PARTICIPLE: देखैत *dĕkhait.*

PAST PARTICIPLE: देखल *dekhal.*

Simple Tenses.

INDICATIVE MOOD.

§ 61a. (*a*)—**Present:** *'I see,' 'I shall see,' &c.*

NOTE.—This tense is frequently used with future signification.

Person.	SINGULAR.		PLURAL.	
	Masculine.	Feminine.	Masculine.	Feminine.
1st	देखलौं *dekhalõ* or देखॅलौं *dekhĕlõ.*		देखीला *dekhílá,* देखीले *dekhíle,* देखॅली *dekhaĭlí,* or देखली *dekhalí.*	
2nd	देखले *dekhale* or देखॅले *dekhĕle.*	देखलिस *dekhalis,* देखॅलिस *dekhĕlis.*	देखलऽ *dekhala* or देखॅलऽ *dekhĕla.*	
3rd	देखला *dekhalá* or देखॅला *dekhĕlá.*		देखले *dekhale,* or देखॅले *dekhĕle,* देखलन्ह *dekhalanh* or देखॅलन्ह *dekhĕlanh.*	देखलिन्ह *dekhalinh* or देखॅलिन्ह *dekhĕlinh.*

Honorific form for second and third persons: देखीले *dekhíle.*

NOTE.—In this tense the vowel of the root always remains long, and is never shortened when antepenultimate.

Concerning the pronunciation of this tense, see § 41.

§ 61b. (a)—Preterite: '*I saw,*' &c.

Person.	Singular.		Plural.	
	Masculine.	Feminine.	Masculine.	Feminine.
1st	देख॰लों *dĕkh'lõ,* देख॰लौं *dĕkh'laũ.*		देख॰ली *dĕkh'li.* देख॰लिऐन्ह *dĕkh'liainh.*	
2nd	देख॰ले *dĕkh'le,* देख॰लस *dĕkh'las.**	देख॰लिस *dĕkh'lis.**	देख॰लह, देख॰लऽ, *dĕkh'lah, dĕkh'la.* देखल॰होक *dekhal'hok.*	देख॰लू *dĕkh'lú.**
3rd	देख॰ले *dĕkh'le.* देख॰लक *dĕkh'lak.* देखल॰कै देखल॰कैक *dĕkhal'kai, dĕkhal'kaik.*		देख॰लन्ह, देख॰लथ *dĕkh'lanh, dĕkh'lath.* देखल॰थिन्ह, देखल॰थुन्ह *dĕkhal'thinh, dĕkhal'thunh.* देखल॰कैन्ह *dĕkhal'kainh.*	देख॰लिन्ह *dĕkh'linh.**

* Bhojpúrí forms, only used in the west of the district.

Honorific forms for first and second persons: देख॰ली *dĕkh'li.*

§ 62. (b)—Future: '*I shall see,*' &c.

Person.	Singular.		Plural.	
	Masculine.	Feminine.	Masculine.	Feminine.
1st	देख्बै, देख्बैक, *dĕkh'bai, dĕkh'baik.* देख्बौ, देख्बौक, *dĕkh'bau, dĕkh'bauk.*		देखब, देख्बैन्ह, *dekhab, dĕkh'bainh.*	
2nd	देख्बे *dĕkh'be.*		देख्बह, देख्बऽ, *dĕkh'bah, dĕkh'ba.*	देख्बू *dĕkh'bú.**
3rd	देखत *dekhat.* देख्तै, देख्तैक, *dĕkh'tai, dĕkh'taik.* देख्तौ, देख्तौक, *dĕkh'tau, dĕkh'tauk.* देखी *dekhi.**		देख्तन्ह *dĕkh'tanh.* देख्तैन्ह *dĕkh'tainh.* देखिहैँ *dĕkhihĕ.**	देख्तिन्ह *dĕkh'tinh.**

* Bhojpúrí forms, only used in the west of the district.

Honorific forms for second and third persons: देखब *dekhab* or देख्बैन्ह *dĕkh'bainh.*

CONJUNCTIVE (CONDITIONAL) MOOD.

§ 63. (c)—Present : '*(If) I see;*' rarely '*I see,*' or '*I shall see,*' *&c.*

Person.	Singular.		Plural.	
	Masculine.	Feminine.	Masculine.	Feminine.
1st	देखू *dekhú.* देखों, देखौं, *dekhõ, dekhaũ.*		देखी, देखिऐन्ह, *dekhí, dĕkhiainh.*	
2nd	देख *dekh,* देखे *dekhe,* देखस *dekhas.**	देखिस *dekhis.**	देखह, देखठ *dekhah, dekha.* देख॰होक *dĕkh'hok.*	देखू *dekhú.**
3rd	देखे *dekhe,* देखो *dekho.* देखै, देखैक, *dekhai, dekhaik.* देखस *dekhas.**		देखथ *dekhath.* देख॰थिन्ह, देख॰थुन्ह, *dĕkh'thinh, dĕkh'thunh* देखैन्ह, देखन्ह, *dekhainh, dekhanh.*	देखिन्ह *dekhinh.*

* Bhojpúrí forms, only used in the west of the district.

Honorific forms for second and third persons : देखी *dekhí* or देखौ *dekhau.*

§ 64. (*d*)—Preterite: '(*If*) *I had seen,*' *&c.*

Person.	Singular. Masculine.	Singular. Feminine.	Plural. Masculine.	Plural. Feminine.
1st	देखन्तौं *děkh'tõ.** देखन्तौँ *děkh'tau͂.*		देखन्ती *děkh'ti.* देखन्तिऐन्ह *děkh'tiainh.*	
2nd	देखन्ते *děkh'te.* देखन्तस *děkh'tas.*†	देखन्तिस *děkh'tis.*†	देखन्तह *děkh'tah.* देखन्तठ *děkh'ta.* देखतन्होक *děkhat'hok.*	देखन्तू *děkh'tú.*†
3rd	देखैत *děkhait* or देखित *dekhit.*		देखन्तथ *děkh'tath.* देखतन्थिन्ह *děkhat'thinh.* देखतन्थुन्ह *děkhat'thunh.* देखन्तन्ह *děkh'tanh.*	देखन्तिन्ह *děkh'tinh.*†

*Or देखितौं *děkhitõ*, and so throughout.

† Bhojpúrí forms, only used in the west of the district.

Honorific forms for second and third persons: देखन्ती *děkh'ti* or देखन्तौ *děkh'tau.*

Imperative Mood

§ 65. (*e*)—Present.—Same as Present Conjunctive.

Precative Forms.

Non-honorific—

2nd person: देखिहठ *děkhiha*, 'you will be good enough to see.'

Honorific—

2nd person: देखू *dekhú*, देखी *dekhi*, देखब *dekhab*, देखिहेँ *děkhihě*, देखिऔ *děkhiau*, 'be good enough to see.' A still more respectful form is देखल जाओ *dekhal jāo.*

(B)—Periphrastic Tenses.

INDICATIVE MOOD.

§ 66. In the following paradigms the optional forms and dialectic forms of the auxiliary verbs will not all be given, as taking up too much valuable space. For similar reasons feminine forms are generally omitted. When not given, they only differ from the masculine in assuming the feminine form of the auxiliary verb. Thus the second singular definite present is—masculine देखैत हए *dĕkhait haë* or देखैत हस *dĕkhait has*, and feminine देखैत हिस *dĕkhait his.*

§ 67. (*g*)—Definite Present: '*I am seeing,*' *&c.*

Person.	Singular.	Plural.
1st	देखैत हउ *dĕkhait haú.*	देखैत हइ *dĕkhait hai.*
2nd	देखैत हए *dĕkhait haë.*	देखैत हऽ *dĕkhait ha.*
3rd	देखैत है *dĕkhait hai.*	देखैत हैन्ह *dĕkhait hainh.*

To form the feminine, use feminine forms of the auxiliary verb. Thus, second singular देखैत हिस *dĕkhait his*, plural देखैत हउ *dĕkhait haú;* third plural देखैत हविन्ह *dĕkhait hawinh.*

Any optional form of the present of the defective auxiliary verb may be used; also any other of the defective auxiliary verbs in the present tense. Thus, first plural, देखैत हती *dĕkhait hati*, देखैत छी *dĕkhait chhi*, देखैत छिकी or छती *dĕkhait chhiki* or *chhati*, देखैत थिकी *dĕkhait thikí*, or (in the west of the district) देखैत बाटी *dĕkhait báṭi.* Before the second and third defective auxiliary verbs the final त *t* of the present participle may optionally be omitted. The participle and auxiliary are then written as one word: thus, first plural देखैछी *dĕkhaichhi*, देखैछिकी *dĕkhaichhiki*, or देखैथिकी *dĕkhaithiki.*

§ 68. (*h*)—By changing the initial छ *chh* of the second auxiliary verb into स *s*, the following somewhat irregular (and in the third person singular the usual) form of the definite present is arrived at:—

Person.	SINGULAR.	PLURAL.
	Masculine and Feminine.	Masculine and Feminine.
1st	*Not used.*	देखैसी *dĕkhaisī.*
2nd	देखैसे *dĕkhaise.*	देखैसऽ *dĕkhaisa.*
3rd	देखैसै *dĕkhaisai.*	देखैसथ *dĕkhaisath.*
	देखैसैक *dĕhhaisaik.*	देखैसैन्ह *dĕkhaisainh.*
	देखैअ *dĕkhaia.*	
	देखैए *dĕkhaie.*	

The feminine is the same as the masculine.

§ 69. (*i*)—Imperfect: '*I was seeing.*'

Person.	Singular.	Plural.
1st	देखैत छलौं *dĕkhait chhalõ.*	देखैत छली *dĕkhait chhalī.*
2nd	देखैत छले *dĕkhait chhale.*	देखैत छलऽ *dĕkhait chhala.*
3rd	देखैत छल *dĕkhait chhal.*	देखैत छलैन्ह *dĕkhait chhalainh.*

To form the feminine, use feminine forms of the auxiliary verb, as in the definite present.

Any optional form of the preterite of the defective auxiliary verb may be used. Also the fifth defective auxiliary verb in the present (preterite) tense: thus, first plural देखैत रही *dĕkhait rahí*. Before the second auxiliary verb the final त *t* of the present participle may optionally be omitted. The participle and auxiliary are then written as one word: thus, first plural देखैछली *dĕkhaichhalí*.

§ 70. (*j*)—Durative Future: '*I shall be seeing,*' *&c.*

Person.	Singular.	Plural.
1st	देखैत होएबैक *dĕkhait hŏĕbaik.*	देखैत होएब *dĕkhait hoĕb.*
2nd	देखैत होएबे *dĕkhait hoĕbe.*	देखैत होएबऽ *dĕkhait hoĕba.*
3rd	देखैत होअत *dĕkhait hoät.*	देखैत होतन्ह *dĕkhait hotaṇh.*

To form the feminine, use feminine forms of the auxiliary verb, as in the definite present.

Any optional form of the future of the complete auxiliary verb may be used throughout.

§ 71. (*k*)—Perfect: '*I have seen,*' *&c.*

This tense has two forms of conjugation, used with equal frequency.

Form I.

Person.	Singular.	Plural.
1st	देखऽलौं छऽ *dĕkh'lŏ ha.*	देखऽली छऽ *dĕkh'lí ha.*
2nd	देखऽले छऽ *dĕkh'le ha.*	देखऽलऽ छऽ *dĕkh'la ha.*
3rd	देखऽलक छऽ *dĕkh'lak ha.*	देखलऽकैन्ह छऽ *dĕkhal'kainh ha.*

To form the feminine, use feminine forms of the preterite: thus, second plural feminine देखऽलू छऽ *dĕkh'lú ha.*

Any optional form of the preterite may be used.

The word हउ *ha* in this tense has a peculiar pronunciation, something like the English word 'haw.'

FORM II.

Person.	Singular.	Plural.
1st	देखऽले हउ *dĕkh'le haú.*	देखऽले हई *dĕkh'le haí.*
2nd	देखऽले हए *dĕkh'le haë.*	देखऽले हऽ *dĕkh'le ha.*
3rd	देखऽले है *dĕkh'le hai.*	देखऽले हैन्ह *dĕkh'le hainh.*

To form the feminine, use feminine forms of the auxiliary verb: thus, second singular feminine देखऽले हिस *dĕkh'le his*, and so on, as in the definite present.

As in the definite present, any optional form of the present of the defective auxiliary verb may be used, and also any other of the defective auxiliary verbs in the present tense: thus, first plural देखऽले हती *dĕkh'le hati*, देखऽले छी *dĕkh'le chhi*, and so on.

§ 72. (*l*)—Pluperfect: '*I had seen*,' &c.

This also, like the perfect, has two forms of conjugation.

FORM I.

Person.	Singular.	Plural.
1st	देखऽलौं रहे *dĕkh'lõ rahe.*	देखऽली रहे *dĕkh'li rahe.*
2nd	देखऽले रहे *dĕkh'le rahe.*	देखऽलऽ रहे *dĕkh'la rahe.*
3rd	देखऽलक रहे *dĕkh'lak rahe.*	देखलऽकैन्ह रहे *dĕkhal'kainh rahe.*

To form the feminine, use feminine forms of the preterite; thus, second plural feminine देखऽलू रहे *dĕkh'lú rahe.*

Any of the other forms of the preterite may be used throughout.

FORM II.

Person.	Singular.	Plural.
1st	देख॰ले छलों *dĕkh'le chhalõ.*	देख॰ले छली *dĕkh'le chhalī.*
2nd	देख॰ले छले *dĕkh'le chhale.*	देख॰ले छल॰ *dĕkh'le chhala.*
3rd	देख॰ले छल *dĕkh'le chhal.*	देख॰ले छलैन्ह *dĕkh'le chhalainh.*

To form the feminine, use feminine forms of the auxiliary, as in the imperfect.

Any optional form of the preterite of the second defective auxiliary verb may be used; also the fifth defective auxiliary verb in the present (preterite) tense: thus, first plural देख॰ले रही *dĕkh'le rahí,* and so on.

§ **73.** (*m*)—**Future Exact:** '*I shall have seen,*' '*I may have seen,*' *&c.*

Person.	Singular.	Plural.
1st	देख॰ले होएबैक *dĕkh'le hŏĕbaik.*	देख॰ले होएब *dĕkh'le hoĕb.*
2nd	देख॰ले होएबे *dĕkh'le hoĕbe.*	देख॰ले होएब॰ *dĕkh'le hoĕba.*
3rd	देख॰ले होअत *dĕkh'le hoăt.*	देख॰ले होतन्ह *dĕkh'le hotanh.*

To form the feminine, use feminine forms of the auxiliary verb, as in the definite present.

Any other form of the future of the complete auxiliary verb may be used instead throughout.

This corresponds to the second form of the perfect and pluperfect. Sometimes forms corresponding to the first forms of these tenses are also found,—thus देख॰ली होइ *dĕkh'li hoi,* देख॰ल॰ होइ *dĕkh'la hoi, &c.*

CONJUNCTIVE (CONDITIONAL) MOOD.

§ 74. (*n*)—Future Conditional: '*(If) I be seeing,' &c*

Person.	Singular.	Plural.
1st	देखैत होउ *dĕkhait hoú.*	देखैत होई *dĕkhait hoi.*
2nd	देखैत होए *dĕkhait hoe.*	देखैत होअ *dĕkhait hoa.*
3rd	देखैत होऐ *dĕkkait hoai.*	देखैत होऐन्ह *dĕkhait hoainh.*

To form the feminine, use feminine forms of the auxiliary verb.

Any other form of the present of the complete auxiliary verb may be used instead throughout.

§ 75. (*o*)—Durative Present Conditional: '*(If) I were seeing,' &c.*

Person.	Singular.	Plural.
1st	देखैत होइतौं *dĕkhait hoïtõ.*	देखैत होइती *dĕkhaït hoïti.*
2nd	देखैत होइते *dĕkhait hoïte.*	देखैत होइतह *dĕkhaït hoïta.*
3rd	देखैत होइत *dĕkhait hoït.*	देखत होइतन्ह *dĕkhaït hoïtanh.*

To form the feminine, use feminine forms of the auxiliary verb.

Any other form of the preterite conditional of the complete auxiliary verb may be used instead throughout.

§ 76. (*p*)—Future Exact Conditional: '*(If) I have seen,*' *&c.*

Person.	Singular.	Plural.
1st	देख॰ले होउ *dĕkh'le hoú.*	देख॰ले होइ *dĕkh'le hoi.*
2nd	देख॰ले होए *dĕkh'le hoe.*	देख॰ले होअ *dĕkh'le hoa.*
3rd	देख॰ले होऐ *dekh'le hoai.*	देख॰ले होऐन्ह *dĕkh'le hoainh.*

To form the feminine, use feminine forms of the auxiliary verb.

Any other form of the present of the complete auxiliary verb may be used instead throughout.

§ 77. (*q*)—Preterite Conditional: '*(If) I had seen,*' *&c.*

Person.	Singular.	Plural.
1st	देख॰ले होइतौँ *dĕkh'le hoïtò.*	देख॰ले होइती *dĕkh'le hoïti.*
2nd	देख॰ले होइते *dĕkh'le hoi:e.*	देख॰ले होइतह *dĕkh'le hoïta.*
3rd	देख॰ले होइत *dĕkh'le hoït.*	देख॰ले होइतन्ह *dĕkh'le hoïtanh.*

To form the feminine, use feminine forms of the auxiliary verb.

Any other form of the preterite conditional of the complete auxiliary verb may be used instead throughout.

§ 78. Participles.

ADJECTIVAL.

Present, 'seeing' .... { देखित *dekhit.* / देखैत *dĕkhaït.* }

Past, 'seen' .... { *a)* देखल *dekhal.* / *b)* देखल भेल *dekhal bhel.* }

CONJUNCTIVE.

'Having seen' .... देख* के *dekh kĕ* or देख* कठ *dekh ka.*

§ 79. Infinitives or Verbal Nouns, '*to see,*' '*the act of seeing.*'

Nominative.	Oblique.
देख *dekh.**	देखे *dekhĕ.*
देखल *dekhal.*	देखन्ला *dĕkh'lá.*
देखब *dekhab.*	*Wanting.*†

§ 80. Noun of Agency, '*one who sees.*'

देखनिहार *dĕkh'nihár* or देखन्वैया *dĕkh'waiyá.*

---

* This form of the verbal noun is always the same as the root. In poetry it sometimes takes the form देखि *dekhi.* So also in the conjunctive participle.

† The oblique form of this verbal noun is not used. Judging from analogy of other dialects, we should expect देखन्बा *dĕkh'bá.*

CHAPTER VII.

THE REGULAR NEUTER VERB.

§ 81. This verb differs from the active verb only in the formation of certain of its past tenses. The three more usual past tenses are here given; the conjugation of the rest of the verb can be learnt from the conjugation of the √ देख *dekh*.

NOTE that throughout the periphrastic tenses of the neuter verb, in which the past participle occurs, the past participle takes the direct form गिरल *giral*, not the oblique form गिरले *gir'lĕ*, which might be expected: thus हम गिरल होएब *ham giral hoeb*, 'I shall have fallen,' and not हम गिरले होएब *ham gir'le hoĕb*, 'I shall have fallen.'

§ 82. √ गिर *gir*, 'fall.'

PAST PARTICIPLE: गिरल *giral*.

INDICATIVE MOOD.

§ 83. (*a*) Preterite: '*I fell*' *&c.*

Person.	Singular.		Plural.	
	Masculine.	Feminine.	Masculine.	Feminine.
1st	गिर॰लोँ *gir'lō*, गिर॰लौँ [*gir'lāũ*.		गिर॰ली *gir'lī*.	
			गिर॰लिऐन्ह *gir'liainh*.	
2nd	गिर॰ले, *gir'le*.		गिर॰लह *gir'lah*. गिर॰लऽ *gir'la*.	गिर॰लू, *gir'lú*.*
	गिर॰लस *gir'las*.*	गिर॰लिस *gir'lis*.*	गिरल॰होक *giral'hok*.	
3rd	गिरल *giral*, गिर॰ले [*gir'le*.		गिर॰लन्ह *gir'lanh*.	गिर॰लिन्ह *gir'linh*.*
	गिर॰लक *gir'lak*.		गिर॰लथ,-॰थिन्ह,-॰थुन्ह, *gir'lath,-'thinh,-'thunh*.	
	गिर॰लै, गिर॰लैक, *gir'lai*, *gir'laik*.		गिर॰लैन्ह *gir'lainh*.	
	गिर॰लौ, गिर॰लौक, *gir'lau*, *gir'lauk*.			

* Bhojpúrí forms, only used in the west of the district.

§ 84. (*k*)—Perfect: '*I have fallen,*' *&c*

FORM I.

Person.	Singular.	Plural.
1st	गिर॰लोँ हऽ *gir'lõ ha.*	गिर॰ली हऽ *gir'lī ha.*
2nd	गिर॰ले हऽ *gir'le ha.*	गिर॰लऽ हऽ *gir'la ha.*
3rd	गिरल हऽ *giral ha.*	गिर॰लन्ह हऽ *gir'lanh ha.*

To form the feminine, use feminine forms of the preterite: thus, second plural feminine गिर॰लू हऽ *gir'lū ha.*

Any of the other forms of the preterite may be used throughout.

The word हऽ *ha* in this tense has a peculiar pronunciation, something like that of the English word 'haw.'

FORM II.

This form means, '*I am fallen,*' rather than '*I have fallen.*'

Person.	Singular.	Plural.
1st	गिरल हऊ *giral haŭ.*	गिरल हई *giral haĭ.*
2nd	गिरल हए *giral haë.*	गिरल हऽ *giral ha.*
3rd	गिरल है *giral hai.*	गिरल हैन्ह *giral hainh.*

To form the feminine, use feminine forms of the auxiliary; thus, second singular feminine गिरल हिस *giral his*, and so on.

Any optional form of the present of the defective auxiliary verb may be used, and also any of the defective auxiliary verbs in the present tense: thus, गिरल हती *giral hati*, गिरल छी *giral chhí*, &c.

§ 85. (*l*)—Pluperfect: '*I had fallen*,' &c.

FORM I.

Person.	Singular.	Plural.
1st	गिर॰लौँ रहे *gir'lõ rahe.*	गिर॰ली रहे *gir'lí rahe.*
2nd	गिर॰ले रहे *gir'le rahe.*	गिर॰लऽ रहे *gir'la rahe.*
3rd	गिरल रहे *giral rahe.*	गिर॰लन्ह रहे *gir'lanh rahe.*

To form the feminine, use feminine forms of the preterite: thus, second plural feminine गिर॰लू रहे *gir'lú rahe.*

Any of the other forms of the preterite may be used throughout.

FORM II.

This form means '*I was fallen*,' rather than '*I had fallen*.'

Person.	Singular.	Plural.
1st	गिरल छलौँ *giral chhalõ.*	गिरल छली *giral chhalí.*
2nd	गिरल छले *giral chhale.*	गिरल छलऽ *giral chhala.*
3rd	गिरल छल *giral chhal.*	गिरल छलैन्ह *giral chhalainh.*

To form the feminine, use feminine forms of the auxiliary: thus, second plural feminine गिरल छलू *giral chhalú*, and so on.

Any optional form of the preterite of the second auxiliary verb may be used; also the fifth auxiliary verb in the present (preterite) tense: thus, first plural गिरल रही *giral rahí*, and so on.

CHAPTER VIII.

VOOALIO ROOTS.

§ 86. **Many verbs have roots ending in vowels, and the junction of the root with the termination frequently causes some slight apparent irregularity.**

For this reason the following examples are given of the conjugation of verbs having roots ending in vowels. They are here conjugated in the masculine gender, and through the four radical and participial tenses. From these the periphrastic tenses can easily be formed. It has not been thought necessary to give the conjugation in full for each person.

With regard to the shortening of the root-vowel, see General Introduction, § 36.

§ 87. Example of a verb whose root ends in आ *á* :—

The conjugation of these verbs should be carefully studied, as a large class of active and causal verbs follows it.

In the preterite indicative these verbs insert a junction vowel between the root and the ल *l* of the termination: thus ख* + ए + लौँ *kha* + *ĕ* + *lō*, or खैलौँ *khailō*, 'I ate,' where ए *ĕ* is the junction vowel; and प* + उ + लौँ *pa* + *u* + *lō*, or पौलौँ *paulĕ*, 'T got,' where उ *u* is the junction vowel. As will be subsequently seen, the same peculiarity exists in other tenses besides the preterite.

The following rules show when ए *ĕ* and when उ *u* is the junction vowel :—

1) All active (including causal) verbs take उ *u*: thus पौलौँ* *paulō* 'I got;' चढ़ौलौँ *chaṛhaulō*, 'I caused to ascend.'

Exception.—The root √ खा *khá*,* 'eat,' always takes ए *ĕ*: thus खैलौँ *khailĕ*, 'I ate.'

---

* With regard to the shortening of the root-vowel and contraction of concurrent vowels, see General Introduction, §§ 34, 36.

2) All neuter verbs take ए ĕ: thus अघैलों *aghailõ*, 'I was satiated.'

Exception.—The √ गा *gá*, 'sing,' always takes उ *u*: thus गौलों *gaulõ*, 'I sang.'

It is usual to add the letter व *w* to the end of all roots which take उ *u*, in order to distinguish them from those which take the letter ए *ĕ*: thus √ पाव *paw*, √ गाव *gáw*, *&c.*, which take उ *u*; but √ अघा *aghá*, आ *á*, *&c.*, which take ए *ĕ*.

Note.—The √ आ *á*, 'come,' is irregular, in that it takes उ *u* as its junction vowel in the Bhojpúrí present indicative, the present participle, and the preterite conjunctive, while it takes ए *ĕ* as its junction vowel in the preterite indicative and connected forms.

All verbs which take a उ *u* in the preterite indicative insert a व *w* in the past participle; and similarly all verbs which take ए *e*, insert it also in the past participle and in that form of the 3rd singular preterite which is the same as the past participle.

All these verbs, without exception, take ए *ĕ* as the junction vowel in the future indicative.

§ 88. The following examples will make the above remarks clear.

The easiest way of remembering these changes is to note the form of the past participle of each verb; and then, as explained in General Introduction, § 37, the व *wa* or ऍ *ĕ* is weakened in certain cases to उ *u* or इ *i* respectively.

Many people write इ *i* instead of ऍ *ĕ*: thus अइलौं *aïlõ*, instead of अऍलौं *aĕlõ*. The word for 'he came' is always आऍल *áĕl*, and never आइल *áïl*. See § 96.

Many people also write ओ *ŏ* instead of व *wa* in the past participle. Thus, it is quite common to find the words in the second column of the opposite table spelt पाओल *páŏl*, बजाओल *bajáŏl*, चढ़ाओल *charháŏl*, गाओल *gáŏl*.

§ 89. √ पा *pá*, 'get.'

INFINITIVE (1ST FORM): पा *pá*; obl. पाऍ *páĕ*, पावे *páwĕ*, पावऽ *páwa*, or पा *pá*.

„ (2ND FORM): पावल *páwal*; obl. पौला *paulá*.* (See General Introduction, § 37.)

„ (3RD FORM): पाऍब *páĕb*, 'to get.'

PRES. PART. पावित *páwit* or पवैत *pawait*.†

INDICATIVE MOOD.

Person.	PRETERITE. (See remarks above.)		FUTURE.	
	Singular.	Plural.	Singular.	Plural.
1st	पौलौं *paulõ*.	पौली *paulí*.	पैबैक *paibaik*.	पाऍब *páĕb*.
2nd	पौले *paule*.	पौलऽ *paula*.	पैबे *paibe*.	पैबऽ *paiba*.
3rd	पौलक *paulak*.	पौलन्ह *paulanh*.	पाइ or पावत *pái* or *páwat*.‡	पैहें *paihẽ*. पौतन्ह *pautanh*.

* But from √ खा *khá*, खाऍल *kháĕl*, obl. खैला *khailá*, and so also in other verbs whose junction vowel is ऍ *ĕ*.

† But from √ खा *khá*, खाइत *kháït* or खात *khát*, and so also in other verbs whose junction vowel is ऍ *ĕ*, except √ आ *á*, 'come,' which makes आवित *áwit* or अवैत *await*.

‡ But खाइ *khái* or खात *khát*, and so also in other verbs whose junction vowel is ऍ *ĕ*

BHOJPÚRÍ PRESENT INDICATIVE.

1st. sing. पावेलों *páwělõ*, [but from √ खा *khá*, खालों *khálõ* or खाइलों *kháïlõ*.
2nd do. पावेले *páwěle* . . . . खाले *khále* or खाइले *kháïle*.
3rd do. पावेला *páwělá* . . . . खाला *khálá* or खाइला *kháïlá*.
1st pl. पाईला *páïlá* . . . . खाईला *kháïlá*.
2nd do. पावेलऽ *páwěla* . . . . खालऽ *khála* or खाइलऽ *kháïla*.
3rd do. पावेले *páwěle* . . . . खाले *khále* or खाइले *kháïle*.

It will be seen that verbs which take ए *ě* as the junction vowel drop the syllable वे *wě* in this tense. The only exception is the √ आ *á*, 'come,' which makes आवेलों *áwělõ*, आवेले *áwěle*, &c.

CONDITIONAL MOOD.

Person.	PRESENT.		PRETERITE.	
	Singular.	Plural.	Singular.	Plural.
1st	पाऊ *páú.*	पाईं *páí.*	पौतों *pautõ.**	पौती *pautí.*
2nd	पावे *páwe.*	पावऽ *páwa.*	पौते *paute.*	पौतऽ *pauta.*
3rd	पावै *páwai.*	पावथ *páwath.*	पवैत *pawait.*	पौतन्ह *pautanh.*

* But from √ खा *khá*, खैतों *khaitõ* or खातों *khátõ*, and so on throughout (the third singular being खाइत *kháït* or खात *khát*) for all verbs whose junction vowel is ए *ě*, except the √ आ *á*, 'come.'

To recapitulate,—

It will be seen that verbs whose junction vowel is ए *ě* omit व *w* in the Bhojpúrí present indicative, the present participle, and the preterite conditional. In these forms also they optionally insert इ *i*. The only exception is the √ आ *á*, 'come,' which retains the व *w* in these cases, though it takes ए *ě*, and not उ *u*, in the past participle and tenses formed therefrom. In short, the √ आ *á* is conjugated like a verb whose junction vowel is उ *u* in the present indicative, the present participle, and its derived forms, but like a verb whose junction vowel is ए *ě* in the past participle and its derived forms.

§ 90. Example of a verb whose root ends in ई *í*:—

√पी *pí*, 'drink.'

INFINITIVE (2ND FORM): पीअल *píal* or पील *píl*, 'to drink.'

PRES. PART. पिवैत *piwait* or पीत *pít*.

INDICATIVE MOOD.

Person.	Preterite.		Future.	
	Singular.	Plural.	Singular.	Plural.
1st	पीलौं *pílō*.	पीली *píli*.	पिअबैक *piabaik*.*	पीअब *píab*.*
2nd	पीले *píle*.	पीलऽ *píla*.	पीअबे *píabe** or पीबे [*píbe*.	पीअबऽ *píaba** or [पीबऽ *píba*.
3rd	पीलक *pílak*.	पीलन्ह *pílanh*.	पीअत *píat* or पीत *pít*.	पीअतन्ह *píatanh* or पीतन्ह *pítanh*.

* Often written पीँग्बैक *pičbaik*, पीग्ब *píčb*, &c.

CONDITIONAL MOOD.

Person.	Present.		Preterite.	
	Singular.	Plural.	Singular.	Plural.
1st	पीऊ *piú*.	पी ई *píí*.	पीतौं *pítō*.	पीती *píti*.
2nd	पीए *píe* or पीवे [*píwe*.	पीअ *pía* or पीवऽ *píwa*.	पीते *píte*.	पीतऽ *píta*.
3rd	पीऐ *píai* or पीवै [*píwai*.	पीऐन्ह or पीवैन्ह *píainh* or *píwainh*. पीअथ *píath* or पीवथ [*píwath*.	पिवैत *piwait* or पीत *pít*.	पिवैतन्ह *piwaitanh*, पीतन्ह *pítanh*, or पीतथ *pítath*.

§ 91. Example of a verb whose root ends in ऊ *ú*:—

√ चू *chú*, 'drip.'

INFINITIVE (2ND FORM): चूअल *chúal*, 'to drip.'

PRES. PART. चूइत *chúit* or चुऐत *chuait*.

INDICATIVE MOOD.

Person.	Preterite.		Future.	
	Singular.	Plural.	Singular.	Plural.
1st	चूलौँ *chúlõ*.	चूली *chúli*.	चुअबैक *chuabaik*.	चूअब *chúab*.
2nd	चूले *chúle*.	चूल० *chúla*.	चूबे *chúbe*.	चूब० *chúba*.
3rd	चूअल *chúal*, चुलै [*chulai*.	चूलन्हि *chúlanh* चूलथ *chúlath*.	चूअत *chúat*, चूई *chúi*.	चूतन्हि *chútanh*, चूइहेँ *chúihẽ*.

CONDITIONAL MOOD.

Person.	Present.		Preterite.	
	Singular.	Pl ral.	Singular.	Plural.
1st	चूऊ *chúú*.	चूइ *chúí*.	चूतौँ* *chútõ*.	चूती *chúti*.
2nd	चूए *chúe*.	चूअ *chúa*.	चूते *chúte*.	चूत० *chúta*.
3rd	चूऐ *chúai*.	चूऐन्हि *chúainh* चूअथ *chúath*.	चूइत *chúit*, चुऐत [*chuait*.	चूतन्हि *chútanh*, चूतथ *chútath*.

* Or चूइतौँ *chuitõ*, and so on throughout.

§ 92. Example of a verb whose root ends in ओ *o*:—

√ रो *ro*, 'weep.'

INFINITIVE (2ND FORM): रोअब *roab*, 'to weep.'
PRES. PART. रोइत *roït* or रोऐत *rŏait*.

INDICATIVE MOOD.

Person.	Preterite.		Future.	
	Singular.	Plural.	Singular.	Plural.
1st	रोअलौँ *roälõ.**	रोअली *roäli.*	रोअबैक *rŏäbaik.*†	रोअब *roab.*
2nd	रोअले *roäle.*	रोअलꣳ *roäla.*	रोअबे *roäbe.*	रोअबꣳ *roäba.*
3rd	रोअल *roäl.*	रोअलन्ह *roälanh.* रोअलथ *roälath.*	रोअत, रोएत, रोई, *roät, roĕt, roi.*	रोअतन्ह, रोइहें, *roätanh, roïhē.*

* Or रोएलौँ *rŏĕlõ*, and so throughout.
† रोएबैक *rŏĕbaik*, and so throughout the first and second persons.

CONDITIONAL MOOD.

Person.	Present.		Preterite.	
	Singular.	Plural.	Singular.	Plural.
1st	रोऊ *roú.*	रोई *roi.*	रोइतौँ *roïtõ.*	रोइती *roïti.*
2nd	रोए *roe.*	रोअ *roa.*	रोइते *roïte.*	रोइतꣳ *roïta.*
3rd	रोऐ *roai.*	रोऐन्ह, रोअथ. *roainh, roath.*	रोऐत *rŏait.*	रोइतन्ह *roïtanh.*

For further examples of verbs of this class, see conjugation of √ हो *ho*, § 53 & ff. This root √ रो *ro* is not much used in Southern Maithilí, the √ कान *kán* being preferred. It is, however, given as an example for the sake of uniformity with the other Grammars of this series.

CHAPTER IX.

IRREGULAR VERBS.

§ 93. The following verbs are irregular only in their preterite tens indicative :— √ कर *kar*, 'do ;' √ धर *dhar*, 'seize' or 'place ;' √ हो *ho*, 'become ;' and √ जा *já*, 'go.' Their conjugation is therefore given in that tense only.

The conjugation of √ हो *ho* has been already given in § 53 and ff., and is not given here.

The verbs √ मर *mar*, 'die,' √ दे *de*, 'give,' and √ ले *le*, 'take,' are more or less irregular throughout the tenses, especially the preterite indicative and present conditional. The verbs √ मर *mar* and √ दे *de* are therefore given conjugated throughout the four radical and participial tenses. The verb √ ले *le* is conjugated precisely like the verb √ दे *de*.

§ 94. √कर *kar*, 'do.'

INFINITIVE (2ND FORM) : करल *karal*, कैल *kail*, कइल *kaïl* or कएल *kaĕl*.

PRES. PART. करैत *karait*.

PAST PART. कैल *kail*, कइल *kaïl*, or कएल *kaĕl*.

√धर *dhar*, 'seize,' 'place.'

INFINITIVE (2ND FORM) : धरल *dharal*, धैल *dhail*, धइल *dhaïl* or धएल *dhaĕl*.

PRES. PART. धरैत *dharait*.

PAST. PART. धैल *dhail*, धइल *dhaïl*, or धएल *dhaĕl*.

INDICATIVE MOOD.

Person.	√ कर *kar*, PRETERITE.		√ धर *dhar*, PRETERITE.	
	Singular.	Plural.	Singular.	Plural.
1st	कैलों *kailō.**	कैली *kailī.*	धैलों *dhailō.*†	धैली *dhailī.*
2nd	कैले *kaile.*	कैलऽ *kaila.*	धैले *dhaile.*	धैलऽ *dhaila.*
3rd	कैलक *kailak.*	कैलन्ह *kailanh.*	धैलक *dhailak.*	धैलन्ह *dhailanh.*

* Or कइलों *kaïlō* or कएलों *kaělō*, and so throughout.

† Or धइलों *dhaïlō* or धएलों *dhaělō*, and so throughout.

The following forms of the conjunctive participle should be noted:—

कऽ कऽ *ka ka* or कै कऽ *kai ka*, 'having done.'	धऽ कऽ *dha ka* or धै कऽ *dhai ka*, 'having seized' or 'placed.'

§ 95. √ मर *mar*, 'die.'

VERBAL NOUN (2ND FORM): मरल *maral* or मुअल *mual.*
PRES. PART. „ मरैत *marait* or मुऐत *muait.*
PAST. PART. „ मरल *maral* or मुअल *mual.*

INDICATIVE MOOD.

Person.	PRETERITE (FORM I).		PRETERITE (FORM II).	
	Singular.	Plural.	Singular.	Plural.
1st	मर्लों *mar'lō.*	मर्ली *mar'lī.*	मुअलों *mualō.*	मुअली *mualī.*
2nd	मर्ले *mar'le.*	मर्लऽ *mar'la.*	मुअले *muale.*	मुअले *muale.*
3rd	मरल *maral.*	मर्लैन्ह *mar'lainh.*	मुअल *mual.*	मुअलन्ह *mualanh*

The future indicative is quite regular: thus, first singular मर्बैक *mar'baik*, &c.

CONDITIONAL MOOD.

Person.	PRESENT (FORM I).		PRESENT (FORM II).	
	Singular.	Plural.	Singular.	Plural.
1st	मरू *marú.*	मरी *marí.*	मुऊ *muú.*	मुई *muí.*
2nd	मरे *mare.*	मरऽ *mara.*	मुए *mue.*	मुअ *mua.*
3rd	मरै *marai.*	मरैन्ह *marainh.*	मुऐ *muai.*	मुऐन्ह *muainh.*

Person.	PRETERITE (FORM I).		PRETERITE (FORM II).	
	Singular.	Plural.	Singular.	Plural.
1st	मरितौं *maritõ.*	मरिती *mariti.*	मुइतौं *muitõ.*	मुइती *muití.*
2nd	मरिते *marite.*	मरितऽ *marita.*	मुइते *muite.*	मुइतऽ *muita.*
3rd	मरैत *marait.*	मरितन्ह *maritanh.*	मुऐत *muait.*	मुइतन्ह *muitanh.*

§ 96. √जा *já*, 'go.'

This root is conjugated like √खा *khá* in all tenses but the preterite indicative, which is therefore here given. (See § 87 and ff.) With it is given the same tense of √आ *á*, 'come,' for the sake of comparison.

VERBAL NOUN (2ND FORM) : आएल *áĕl.*	जाएब *jáĕi* or गेल *gel.*
PAST. PART. आएल *áĕl.*	गेल *gel.*

Person.	√आ *á*, PRETERITE INDICATIVE.		√जा *já*, PRETERITE INDICATIVE.	
	Singular.	Plural.	Singular.	Plural.
1st	ऐलौं *ailõ.*	ऐली *ailí.*	गेलौं *gelõ.*	गेली *gelí.*
2nd	ऐले *aile.*	ऐलऽ *aila.*	गेले *gele.*	गेलऽ *gela.*
3rd	आएल *áĕl.*	ऐलैन्ह *ailainh.*	गेल *gel.*	गेलैन्ह *gĕlainh.*

§ 97. √दे *de*, 'give.'

VERBAL NOUN (2ND FORM): देल *del*, 'to give.'

PRES. PART. देत *det*, देइत *deït*, or दैत *dait*.

PAST PART. देल *del*.

INDICATIVE MOOD.

Person.	PRETERITE.		FUTURE.	
	Singular.	Plural.	Singular.	Plural.
1st	देलोँ *delõ*.	देली *deli*.	देबैक *dĕbaik*.	देब *deb*.
2nd	देले *dele*.	देलह *dela*.	देबे *debe*.	देबह *deba*.
3rd	देलक *delak*.	देलन्ह *delanh*.	दी *di* or देत *det*.	दीहेँ or देतन्ह *díhẽ* or *detanh*.

BHOJPÚRÍ PRESENT INDICATIVE.

1st sing. देलोँ *delõ*; 1st pl. देइला *deilá*.

CONDITIONAL MOOD.

Person.	PRESENT.		PRETERITE.	
	Singular.	Plural.	Singular.	Plural.
1st	दीऊ *díú*.	दी *dí*.	देतोँ *detõ* or दितोँ *ditõ*.	देती *deti*.
2nd	दे *de* or देस *des*.	दह *da*.	देते *dete* or दिते *dite*.	देतह *deta*, दितह *dita*.
3rd	दे *de*, देवे *dewe*, or देऐ *deai*.	देऐन्ह or देथ *deainh* or *deth*.	देत *det*, देइत *deït*, दीत *dít*, or दैत *dait*.	देतन्ह *detanh* or दितन्ह *ditanh*.

PRECATIVE: दीहह *díha*, दीही *díhi*, दीऊ *díú*.

Similarly is conjugated the √ले *le*, 'take,' the letter ल *la* being substituted for the letter द *da* throughout.

CHAPTER X.

THE PASSIVE VERB.

§ 98. The passive verb is formed by conjugating the verbal noun ending in अल *al* with the verb √जा *já*, 'go:' thus देखल जाएल *dekhal jáël* 'to be seen.' This verbal noun is not altered for gender, number, person, or tense, only the verb जाएल *jáël* being conjugated. Thus—

Indicative Preterite Masculine: '*I was seen*,' *&c.*

Person.	Singular.	Plural.
1st	देखल गेलौं *dekhal gelõ.*	देखल गेली *dekhal geli.*
2nd	देखल गेले *dekhal gele.*	देखल गेलह *dekhal gela.*
3rd	देखल गेल *dekhal gel.*	देखल गेलैन्ह *dekhal gĕlainh.*

§ 99. This verbal noun in अल *al* must be carefully distinguished from the past participle having the same termination. The former even in irregular verbs is sometimes quite regular, so that we have verbal nouns such as जाएल *jáël* and करल *karal,* besides past participles like गेल *gel* and कैल *kail.* The only exceptions are √दे *de* and √ले *le,* for which see the full conjugation of the former verb. At the same time it must be remembered that the verbal noun can also take the form of the past participle as well as its proper form: so that we may have गेल *gel* and कैल *kail* as verbal nouns as well as जाएल *jáël* and करल *karal.* An example of an irregular passive verb is जाएल जाइअ *jáël jáïa* (impersonal), 'it is gone'—'*itum est;*' but, used in the sense of the potential, 'it can go.' When neuter verbs are used in the passive voice, they are always used in an impersonal potential sense: thus, हम॰रा से चलल नह जाइअ *ham'rá se chalal na jäïa*, 'by me it cannot be gone,' *i.e.* 'I cannot go.'

§ 100. Another common form of the passive is made by adding to the direct form of the first variety of the verbal noun (which is the same in form as the root) the verb परल *paral*, 'to fall;' the whole then forms an intensive compound. (See § 114.)

Examples of this form are—

कुछु कुछु जान परैत हऽ *kuchhu kuchhu ján parait ha*, 'a little is evidənt,' *i.e.* 'it is slightly apparent.'

एकऽरा से ई बूझ परैअ *ĕk'rá se ĭ búјh paraia*, ·ırom this, this is understood.'

कुछु ऊँच नऽ देख परैअ *kuchhu úch na dekh paraia*, 'it is not seen to be at all increased in size.'

§ 101. The Potential Passive Voice.

The voice is formed by adding आ *á* to the root: thus √ देख *dekh*, potential passive देखा *dekhá*. देखा *dekhá* is then conjugated exactly like any intransitive verb in आ *á*, as explained in § 88. It thus differs from the causal verb (see § 103), which adds आव *áw* to the root. The potential passive is conjugated quite regularly, the following being its principal parts, with which the corresponding causal forms are given for the sake of comparison.

	POTENTIAL PASSIVE.	CAUSAL.
Root	देखा *dekhá*.	देखाव *dĕkháw*.
Infinitive, 2nd form ...	देखाएल *dĕkháĕl*; obl. देखैला *dĕkhailá*.	देखावल *dĕkháwal*; obl. देखौला *dĕkhaulá*.
Past part. ...	देखाएल *dĕkháĕl*.	देखावल *dĕkháwal*.
1st pl. pret. ind. ...	देखैली *dĕkhailĭ*.	देखौली *dĕkhaulĭ*.
2nd sing. pret. ind. ...	देखैले *dĕkhaile*.	देखौले *dĕkhaule*.
2nd pl. pret. ind. ...	देखैलऽ *dĕkhaila*.	देखौलऽ *dĕkhaula*.
3rd sing. pret. ind. ...	देखाएल *dĕkháĕl*.	देखौलक *dĕkhaulak*.
3rd pl. pret. ind. ...	देखैलन्ह *dĕkhailanh*.	देखौलन्ह *dĕkhaulanh*.
Bhojpúrí.		
2nd pl. pres. ind. ...	देखालऽ *dĕkhála*.	देखावेलऽ *dĕkháwĕla*.
3rd pl. pres. ind. ...	देखाले *dĕkhále*.	देखावेले *dĕkháwĕle*.

It will be observed that the potential passive verb shortens its antepenultimate, as occurs in the case of causals. (See § 104.)

There is a tendency, which amounts almost to a rule, to drop the junction vowel in in the conjugation of the tenses not derived from the past participle of the potential passive. Thus we get the following forms:—

	Usual forms, dropping the junction vowel.	Regular forms, according to § 89.
Infinitive, 3rd form	देखाब *dĕkháb.*	देखाएब *dĕkháĕb.*
1st pl. fut. ...	देखाब *dĕkháb.*	देखाएब *dĕkháĕb.*
2nd pl. fut. ...	देखाबठ *dĕkhába.*	देखैबठ *dĕkhaiba.*
1st pl. pret. conj. ...	देखाती *dĕkháti.*	देखैती *dĕkhaiti.*
3rd pret. conj. and pres. part.	देखात *dĕkhát.*	देखाइत *dĕkháït.*

The potential passive has a peculiar force, intimating, not that a thing *is* done, but that it *can be* done. Thus ई पोथी पढ़ाइच *i pothi parháïa,* 'this book *can be* read,' but ई पोथी पढ़ल जाइच *i pothí parhal jáïa,* 'this book is being read.'

§ 102. The Periphrastic Passive Voice.

A very common kind of passive voice is formed by placing the verb √ आ *á* after the first or shortest form of a verbal noun in the locative case: thus देखे में आएल *dekhĕ mĕ áĕl,* 'the coming into seeing,' *i.e.* 'to be seen.' The person by whom the action is done is put in the oblique genitive form of the noun or pronoun when there is one: thus तोँ हमऽरा देखेँ मेँ ऐलऽ *tŏ ham'rá dekhĕ mẽ aila,* 'you came into my seeing,' 'you were seen by me.' The following example shows a verb in this voice conjugated in the present indicative masculine:—

Singular.	Plural.
1. देखेँ मेँ अवैछी *dekhĕ mẽ awaichhi.*	1. देखेँ मेँ अवैछी *dekhĕ mẽ awaichhi.*
2. देखेँ मेँ अवैछे *dekhĕ mẽ awaichhe.*	2. देखेँ मेँ अवैछऽ *dekhĕ mẽ awaichha.*
3. देखेँ मेँ अवैअ *dekhĕ mẽ awaia.*	3. देखेँ मेँ अवैछथ *dekhĕ mẽ awaichhath.*

EXAMPLE.—हमऽरा सभ तोहऽरा देखेँ मेँ अवैछी *ham'rá sabh tŏh'rá dekhĕ mẽ awaichhí,* 'we are seen by you.'

CHAPTER XI.

CAUSAL VERBS.

§ 103. A causal verb is formed by adding आव *áw* to the root of the simple verb, and a double causal by adding वाव *wáw*. The stems thus formed are conjugated exactly like verbs whose roots end in आव *áw*. (See § 87.) The long vowel of आव *áw* and वाव *wáw* is, as usual, liable to be shortened in the antepenultimate (see General Introduction, § 36); and if the व *wa* is followed by the neutral vowel, it becomes उ *u* (see General Introduction, § 37), which with a preceding अ *a* (see General Introduction, § 35) may be written औ *au*.

Thus, taking the simple verb √ उठ *uṭh*, 'rise,' the first plural definite present indicative of its causal would be regularly उठ्वैछी *uṭh'waichhi*. But the first plural preterite would be उठव्ली *uṭhaw'li*, which (as व *wa* is followed by the neutral vowel) becomes (General Introduction, § 37) उठउली *uṭhaüli* or उठौली *uṭhauli*.

Similarly, for the double causal the forms would be उठ्ववैछी *uṭh'wawaichhi* and उठ्वउली *uṭh'waüli*, or उठ्वौली *uṭh'wauli*.

The following are examples of the regular formation of causals and double causals:—

Simple Verb.	Causal.	Double Causal.
√ उठ *uṭh*, 'rise.'	उठाव *uṭháw*, 'raise.'	उठ्वाव *uṭh'wáw*, 'cause to raise.'
√ छिप *chhip*, 'be hidden.'	छिपाव *chhipáw*, 'hide.'	छिप्वाव *chhip'wáw*, 'cause to hide.'
√ नुक *nuk*, 'be hidden.'	नुकाव *nukáw*, 'hide'	नुक्वाव *nuk'wáw*, 'cause to hide.'
√ पक *pak*, 'be cooked.'	पकाव *pakáw*, 'cook.'	पक्वाव *pak'wáw*, 'cause to cook.'

Simple Verb.	Causal.	Double Causal.
मिल *mil*, 'meet.'	मिलाव *miláw*, 'mix.'	मिल॰वाव *mil'wáw*, ['cause to mix.'
सुन *sun*, 'hear.'	सुनाव *sunáw*, 'tell.'	सुन॰वाव *sun'wáw*, 'cause [to tell.'
कह *kah*, 'say.'	कहाव *kaháw*, 'cause [to speak.'	कह॰वाव *kah'wáw*, 'cause [to cause to speak.'

§ 104. If the simple root contains a long vowel it is shortened, vi आ *á* to अ *a*, ई *í* to इ *i*, ऊ *ú* to उ *u*, ए *e* to ऎ *è*, ओ *o* to ऒ *ŏ*, ऐ *ai* to ऐ *aĭ*, an औ *au* to औ *aŭ*.

Similarly, if a root ends in a double consonant, it is made single: thus—

Simple Verb.	Causal.	Double Causal.
जाग *jág*, 'be awake.'	जगाव *jagáw*, 'awaken.'	जग॰वाव *jag'wáw*, 'cause [to awake.'
पाक *pák*, 'be cooked.'	पकाव *pakáw*, 'cook.'	पक॰वाव *pak'wáw*, 'cause [to cook.'
जीत *jít*, 'conquer.'	जिताव *jitáw*, 'cause to.' [conquer.'	जित॰वाव *jit'wáw*, 'cause [to cause to conquer.'
सीख *síkh*, 'learn.'	सिखाव *sikháw*, 'teach.'	सिख॰वाव *sikh'wáw*, 'cause [to teach.'
पी *pí*, 'drink.'	पिआव *piáw*, 'cause to [drink.'	पिअवाव *piawáw*, 'cause [to cause to drink.'
भींज* *bhíj*, 'be wet.'	भिंजाव *bhĭjáw*, 'moisten.'	भिंज॰वाव *bhĭj'wáw*, ['cause to moisten
घूम *ghúm*, 'be turned.'	घुमाव *ghumáw*, 'turn.'	घुम॰वाव *ghum'wáw*, 'cau. [to turn.'

* See General Introduction, § 28.

Simple Verb.	Causal.	Double Causal.
√ बूड़ *búṛ*, 'sink.'	बुड़ाव *buṛáw*, 'immerse.'	बुड़वाव *buṛ'wáw*, 'cause [to immerse.'
√ सूत *sút*, 'sleep.'	सुताव *sutáw*, 'put to [sleep.'	सुतवाव *sut'wáw*, 'cause [to put to sleep.'
√ देख *dekh*, 'see.'	देखाव *děkháw*, 'show.'	देखवाव *děkh'wáw*, 'cause [to show.'
√ बैस *bais*, 'sit.'	बैसाव *baïsáw*, 'seat.'	बैसवाव *baïs'wáw*, 'cause [to sit.'
√ पैँर *paũr*, 'swim.'	पैँराव *paũráw*, 'cause to [swim.'	पैँरवाव *paũr'wáw*, 'cause [to cause to swim.'
√ दौर *daur*, 'run.'	दौराव *daüráw*, 'cause [to run.'	दौरवाव *daür'wáw*, 'cause [to cause to run.'
√ नुक *nukk*, 'be hidden.'	नुकाव *nukáw*, 'hide.'	नुकवाव *nuk'wáw*, 'cause [to hide.'

Note in connection with the above:—

Simple Verb.	Causal.
√ कह *kah*, 'speak'	कहलाव *kah'láw*, also regular.
√ खा *khá*, 'eat'	खिआव *khiáw*.
√ पी *pí*, 'drink'	पिलाव *piláw*, also regular.

§ 105. Some primitive neuter verbs, having a monosyllabic root enclosing a short vowel, form the first causal by simply lengthening that vowel. The double causal is formed in the usual way, *e.g.*—

Simple Verb.	Causal.
√ कट *kaṭ*, 'be cut'	काट *káṭ*, 'cut.'
√ बन्ह *bank*, 'be tied'	बान्ह *bánh*, 'tie.'
√ लद *lad*, 'be loaded'	लाद *lád*, 'load.'
√ खिंच *khiṅch*, 'be dragged'	खीँच * *khích*, 'drag.'

* When the vowel is lengthened, *anuswár* becomes *anunásik*. (Compare General Introduction, § 28.)

§ 106. Sometimes a cognate diphthong is substituted for the long vowel, *e.g.*—

खुल ***khul***, 'be open.'	खोल ***khol***, 'open.'
घुल ***ghul***. 'melt.' (*Neut.*)	घोल ***ghol***, 'melt' (*Act.*)

§ 107. The verb √ निकस *nikas*, 'come out,' makes its causal निकास *nikás*, 'take out,' on the analogy of the above. So also √ पसर *pasar*, 'be scattered,' makes पसार *pasár*, 'scatter,' 'extend;' √ ससर *sasar*, 'slip,' ससार *sasár*, 'cause to slip;' √ उपर *upar*, 'be rooted up,' उपार *upár*, 'root up;' and √ उखर *ukhar*, 'be rooted up,' उखार *ukhár*.

§ 108. The following are irregular :—

Simple Verb.	Causal.	Double Causal.
√ अट *aṭ*, 'be stopped.'	आर *ár*, 'stop.'	अराव *aráw*.
√ फट *phaṭ* or फाट *pháṭ* ['be torn.'	फार *phár*, 'tear.'	फराव *pharáw*.
√ छूट *chhúṭ*, 'be separated.'	छोड़ *chhoṛ* or छाड़ *chháṛ*, 'separate.'	छोड़ाव *chhŏṛáw*.
√ जूट *júṭ*, 'be joined.'	जोड़ *joṛ*, 'join.'	जोड़ाव *jŏṛáw*.
√ टूट *ṭúṭ*, 'be broken.'	तूर *túr* or तूड़ *túṛ*, 'break.'	तुराव *turáw* or तुड़ाव *tuṛáw*.
√ फूट *phúṭ*, 'be burst.'	फोर *phor*, 'burst.'	फोराव *phŏráw*.
√ बिक *bikk*, 'be sold.'	बेँच *bĕch* or बिकाव *bikáw* ['sell.'	बेँचाव *bĕcháw*.
√ रह *rah*, 'remain.'	राख *rákh* or रक्ख *rakkh*, ['place.'	रखाव *rakháw*.
√ मर *mar*, 'die.'	मार *már* or मुआव *muáw*, ['cause to die.'	

CHAPTER XII.

COMPOUND VERBS.

§ 109. Compound verbs are either intensives, potentials, completives, frequentatives, desideratives, continuatives, staticals, inceptives, permissives, or acquisitives.

§ 110. Compound verbs may be classed as—(1) those formed with the verbal noun, and (2) those formed with the participles.

(1) Those formed with the verbal noun are—

a) Intensives.
b) Potentials.
c) Completives.
d) Frequentatives.
e) Desideratives.
f) Inceptives.
g) Permissives.
h) Acquisitives.

(2) Those formed with the participles—

a) Continuatives.
b) Staticals.

Class I.—Compounds formed with the Verbal Noun.*

§ 111. There are three varieties of the verbal noun—

a) In अ *a* (silent), oblique form ए *ĕ*; as देख *dekh*, obl. देखे *dekhĕ.*

b) In अल *al*, oblique form ्ला *'lá*; as देखल *dekhal*, obl. देख्ला *dĕk'lá.*

c) In अब *ab*, oblique form wanting; as देखब *dekhab*, obl. wanting.

The direct first form is always the same as the root.

Compound verbs are either formed with the direct form of the first or second variety of the verbal noun, or with the oblique form of the first variety.

* Much of the succeeding matter is based on Kellogg's Hindí Grammar.

§ 112. *ntensives, Potentials,* and *Completives,* are always formed with the direct form of the first variety; *Frequentatives* are always formed with the direct form of the second variety; and *Desideratives* are generally so. *Inceptives, Permissives,* and *Acquisitives,* are always formed with the oblique form of the first variety.

§ 113. *Intensive* compounds intensify or otherwise modify the meaning of the verb whose root stands first in the compound. They are formed by adding to a verbal noun of the first variety in the direct form one of certain other verbs, which latter verb in conjunction with the verbal noun is then conjugated as usual. This second conjugated member does not, however, retain its separate character and significance, but only modifies, in accordance with the general idea which it embodies, the meaning of the unconjugated verbal noun to which it is annexed. Examples are—

फेँकल *phēkal*, 'to throw.'	फेँक देल *phēk del*, 'to throw away.'
तूरल *túral*, 'to break.'	तूर डालल *túr ḍálal*, 'to break in pieces.'
बनल *banal*, 'to be made.'	बन आएल *ban áĕl* or बन जाएल *ban jáĕl*, ['to be completed.'
खाएल *kháĕl*, 'to eat.'	खा जाएल *khá jáĕl*, 'to eat up.'
बोलल *bolal*, 'to speak.'	बोल उठल *bol uṭhal*, 'to speak suddenly.'
काटल *káṭal*, 'to cut.'	काट लेल *káṭ lel*, 'to cut for oneself.'
राखल *rákhal*, 'to place.'	राख लेल *rákh lel*, 'to lay by.'

§ 114. The auxiliary verbs usually employed to form intensives are—

देल *del*, 'to give,'	implying *intensity.*
डालल *ḍálal*, 'to throw,'	" *violence.*
आएल *áĕl*, 'to come,' } जाएल *jáĕl*, 'to go,' }	" *completion.*
परल *paral*, 'to fall,'	" *chance.*
उठल *uṭhal*, 'to rise,'	" *suddenness.*
लेल *lel*, 'to take,'	" *reflexiveness.*

परल *paral* is also used in intensive compounds to form passives of transitive verbs. (See § 100.)

§ 115. *Potentials* are formed by adding to the same form of the verbal noun of any verb the verb सकल *sakal*, 'to be able,' which may then be conjugated throughout. Examples are—

बोल सकल *bol sakal*, 'to be able to speak.'

ऊ दौर सकैच *ú daur sakaia*, 'he can run.'

हम जा सकब *ham já sakab*, 'I shall be able to go.'

ऊ सभ आ सकथ *ú sabh á sakath*, 'they can come.'

हम नऽ जा सकैछी *ham na já sakaichhí*, 'I cannot go.'

§ 116. *Completives* are formed by adding to the same form of the verbal noun of a verb the verb चुकल *chukal*, 'to be finished,' which may then be conjugated throughout. This compound denotes the *completion* of the act denoted by the primary member of the compound. Examples are—

ऊ खा चुकल *ú khá chukal*, 'he has done eating.'

जब ऊ खा चुकत *jab ú kha chukat*, 'when he shall have eaten.'

ऊ तो जा चुकल हऽ *ú to já chukal ha*, 'he is indeed already gone.'

§ 117. *Frequentatives* are formed by affixing to the direct form of the second variety of the verbal noun of any verb the verb करल *karal*, 'to do.' which may then be used in any tense. Examples are—

आएल करऽ *áĕl kara*, 'come often,' *lit.* 'do the act of coming.'

ऊ कहल करैच *ú kahal karaia*, 'he is in the habit of saying.'

हम शास्त्र के पढ़ल करैत हई *ham sástr ke paṛhal karait haí*, 'I am in the habit of reading the shástras.'

तों हमर बात सभ मानल करऽ *tŏ hamar bát sabh mánal kara*, 'always obey my words.'

तों ऐसन काहे कैल करैत हऽ *tŏ aisan káhĕ kail karait ha*, 'why do you always do so?'

ऊ जाएल करैच *ú jáĕl karaia*, 'he often goes.'

§ 118. ***Desideratives*** are formed, like frequentatives, with the direct form of the verbal noun in अल *al*, substituting the verb चाहल *cháhal*, 'to wish,' for करल *karal* as the second or conjugated member. They denote primarily *desire* to do the action expressed of the principal member; secondarily, the *immediate futurity* of that action. Examples are—

ऊ बोलल चहैछ *ú bolal chahaia*, 'he wishes to speak.'

ऊ मरल चहैत छथ *ú maral chahait hath*, 'he is about to die.'

घड़ी बाजल चहैत रहे *gharí bájal chahait rahe*, 'the clock was on the point of striking.'

Sometimes the principal verb is put in the oblique form of the first variety of the verbal noun with or without the dative postposition के *ke*. Examples are—

ऊ बोलें के चहैछ *ú bolĕ ke chahaia*, 'he wishes to speak.'

ऊ जाए चहैछ *ú jáĕ chahaia*, 'he wishes to go.'

ऊ मरें चहैत छथ *ú marĕ chahait hath*, 'he is about to die.'

The desiderative compound in the precative form is idiomatically used to express obligation or duty. Examples are—

ई पोथी के पढ़ल चाही *í pothí ke paṛhal cháhí*, '(one) ought to read this book.' (*Lit.* 'be good enough to wish to read.')

तोहँरा उहाँ जाए के चहिऔ *tŏh'rá uhá̃ jáĕ ke chahiau*, 'it is right for you (*i.e.* you ought) to go there.'

§ 119. ***Inceptives*** are formed by using the inflected form of the first variety of the verbal noun in construction with the verb लागल *lágal*, 'to be joined,' 'to begin,' and denote the action of the verbal noun as *beginning*. Examples are—

कहें लागल *kahĕ lágal*, 'he began to say.'

मारें लागल *márĕ lágal*, 'he began to beat.'

बाघ खाए लागल *bágh kháĕ lágal*, 'the tiger began to eat.

§ 120. ***Permissives*** are formed by combining the same form of the verbal noun with the verb देल *del*, 'to give,' and express *permission* to do the act denoted by the verbal noun. Examples are—

हमरा जाए दऽ *ham'rá jáě da*, 'let me go.'

हमरा के बोलें दीअ *ham'rá ke bolě díú*, 'be good enough to let me speak.'

ऊ ओकरा के खाए देलक *ú ŏk'rá ke kháě delak*, 'he allowed him to eat.'

§ 121. ***Acquisitives*** are the exact converse of the preceding, and are formed in the same way, substituting पावल *páwal*, 'to get,' for देल *del*. Examples are—

अपने उहाँ जाए न पाएब *ap'ně uhā̃ jáě na páěb*, 'you will not obtain permission to go there.'

हम बैसे ना पौली *ham baisě ná pauli*, 'I was not allowed to sit.'

Class II.—Compounds formed from the Participles.

§ 122. ***Continuatives*** are formed by combining the present participle of any verb with the verbs जाएल *jáěl*, 'to go,' or रहल *rahal*, 'to remain.' The compound with जाएल *jáěl* expresses *steady progression*, and with रहल *rahal* the *continuance* of a complete action. Examples—

ऊ लिखैत जाइत है *ú likhait jáit hai*, 'he is going on writing.'

ऊ छौंड़ी सभ पढ़ैत जाइत रहे *ú chhāũṛí sabh paṛhait jáit rahe*, 'those girls were going on reading.'

पानी बहैत जाइअ *páni bahait jáia*, 'the water keeps flowing away.'

ऊ गवैत रहैअ *ú gawait rahaia*, 'she continues singing.'

तों काहे हसैत रहैत छऽ *tõ káhě hasait rahait chha*, 'why do you keep laughing?'

नदी के धार बहैत रहैअ *nadi kě dhár bahait rahaia*, 'the stream of the river keeps flowing on.'

Closely connected with the above is a common combination in which the past instead of the present participle takes the first place and a verb of motion the second place. An example is—

एक बाघ परल फिरैत रहै *ěk bágh paral phirait rahe*, 'a tiger was prowling about.'

लौँड़ी चलल जाइत रहै *lãũṛí chalal jáit rahe*, 'the girl was going along.'

§ 123. *Staticals* denote motion in a state of doing anything. They are formed by combining a verb of motion with a present participle. Examples are—

ऊ कनैत अवैअ *ú kanait awaia*, 'he comes weeping.'

एक मेँहरारू गवैत अवैत रहै *ěk mĕh'rárú gawait await rahe*, 'a woman was coming singing.'

DIVISION III.

INDECLINABLES.

§ 124. See General Introduction.

APPENDIX I.

The following selections are in the dialect of Central Muzaffarpúr. The fables were translated for me by Rám Charan Lál, Chief Guru in that district. A translation of them and of the conversation will be found in the General Introduction.

SELECTIONS IN THE CENTRAL MUZAFFARPÚR DIALECT.

CONVERSATION BETWEEN TWO VILLAGERS.

१ प्रश्न कहऽ भाइ, कहाँ से अबैत छिकऽ?

उत्तर परऽसौया गाँव से अबैत छिकौ।

२ प्र. उहाँ से कहिया चलऽलऽ?

उ. सबेरे कऽ चलल छौ (or छिकौ)।

३ प्र. कथी ला उहाँ गेल रहऽ?

उ. उहाँ हमर खेत है ओकऽरा देखे गेल रही।

४ प्र. ओइ में की बोअले छिकऽ?

उ. खाली रहऽरि बोअल गेल हऽ।

५ प्र. कहऽ भाइ, एमऽकौ फसिल के की रङ्ग हैक?

उ. एमऽकौ फसिल के हाल की पुछैछी, पानि बरऽसे बिना बड़ बिगरऽता भेल।

६ प्र. आइ काल्ह आहाँ के भाइ नऽ देख परैत छिकथ।

उ. हमर भाइ आइ काल्ह किला में नोकर छथ; एसे बहुत कम अबैत छिकथ।

७ प्र. आइ काल्ह आहाँ के बड़ऽकौ गाय के की हाल है?

उ. ऊ आइ काल्ह गाभिन है, परन्तु घास नऽ मिलें सें दूबर हो गेल है।

८ प्र. कै महिना से गाभिन है?
उ. आठ महिना भेलैक, परन्तु पेट ओकर कुछु ऊँच नऽ देख परैछ।

९ प्र. कोराइ कि अबऽनी नऽ?
उ. हँ, कुछु कुछु जान परैत हऽ।

१० प्र. ई कै बियान है? और कतेक दूध देइछ?
उ. ई एकर आठम बियान है। दू अढ़ाइ सेर दूध एक बेर देइछ।

११ प्र. हमऽरा एक बकऽरी लेवे के है; आहाँ के गाँव मेँ मिलत?
उ. हमऽरा गाँव मेँ बकऽरी सभ तऽ हैक, परन्त दाम महँगा है।

१२ प्र. आहाँ के बकऽरी की भेल?
उ. हम चरे लेल गाँव पर छारऽले रहैत थिकौँ।

१३ प्र. कुछु दूध देइछ?
उ. लरिका सभ के पोए भर हो जाइछै।

१४ प्र. एमऽकी जखि बोएले हऽ कि नऽ?
उ. जखि तऽ बोएली है, परन्तु ओकऽरा मेँ कुछु लाभ नऽ हैक।

१५ प्र. आहाँ कने से चार मोटि मँगऽनी मिल सकैछ?
उ. किअक नऽ? पटौनी भेला पर ले लेबऽ।

१६ प्र. आहाँ कने कतेक मोटि चलैत है?
उ. तीन मोटि तऽ लधऽले छी।

१७ प्र. आहाँ के आम के गाछी कुछु फरैछ की नऽ?
उ. एमऽकी बेर बदऽरी से गाछ सभ मेँ लाही लाग गेल; नऽ तऽ बऊत होइत रहैन्ह।

१८ प्र. थोरे आम हमऽरो अचार के लेल देबऽ?
उ. जब आहाँ के जी चाहे, आ कऽ तुरऽवा लेबऽ।

१९ प्र. आहाँ के लरिका कुछु पढ़ैत है कि नऽ?
उ. हाँ गुरु किहाँ जाइत है; अच्छर तऽ चिन्हऽलक हऽ, आइ काल्ह पहाड़ा पढ़ैत है।

२० प्र. अस्कोल मेँ किअक नऽ भेजी?
उ. कुछु सीख लेओ तब भेजब।

२१ प्र. हमऽहूँ अपऽना लरिका के अस्कोल मेँ भेजे के चहैत छी?
उ. बेस; तऽ हमऽरा लरिका के साथ ओकऽरो के भेज देब।

FABLES.

पहिल बात।

मुसगा आउर मोती के दाना।

एगो मुसगा गोबर के ढेरी के चक्कुर से कोरैत रहै। तब सञ्जोग से ओहि मेँ से एगो बड़ि चुक के मोती निकसऽलैक। मुसगा बाजल जे, वाह वाह कैसन रङ्ग रूप ओ चमक दमक छैक जोहऽरी एकऽरा पवैत, तब बड़ आनन्द होइत परन्तु हमर पेट के आगि ऐसे नऽ बुझाइत। हाए, एक चाउर के दाना हमऽरा हाथ लगैत, तऽ ऐ मोती से बढ़ कऽ रहल। साँच है, जे अप्पन काम नऽ आवै, से चूल्ही भनऽसार मेँ जाए॥

दोसर बात।

कँगाल के पुछऽनाइ आउर फकीर के जवाब देनाइ।

एगो कँगाल, कौनो पहुँचल बाबा जी से पुछलऽकैन्ह जे, हम भूखेँ मरैछी आउर हमर परोसिया गद्दी पर बैसल, बैस कऽ लोटैत है, रात दीन चैन करैत है; ओकऽरा मेँ कौन ऐसन गुन छैक, जे दाता ओकऽरा नेहाल कैलऽथिन्ह, आउर हमऽरा कँगाल बनौलन्ह। ई सुन कऽ बाबा जी कहलऽथिन्ह जे, बाबा, तोँ ई नऽ सुनऽले छऽ कि, भगऽवान झरोखा पर बैस कऽ सभ केउ के मोजऽरा लेइछथ। जेंकर जैसन नोकऽरी रहैछैक, तेकऽरा तैसन देइत छथिन्ह॥

तेसर बात।

देस बिदेस फिरै के लाभ।

कौनो भल मानुस एक बाबा जी से पुछलऽथिन्ह जे, महाराज जी, देस देस गाँवे गाँव भटकऽला से की लाभ है। एक ठाम रह कऽ भगऽवान मेँ किअक नऽ लौ लगऽवैछी कौनो मन्दिर मेँ बइस कऽ दाता के गुन किअक नऽ गवैछी। जोगी जी कहऽलथिन्ह जे बाबा, ई सभ साँच है, मगर तोँ ई कहावत नऽ सुनऽलऽ छऽ कि, बहैत है जे पानि से बड़ुत निर्मल होइत है और बान्हल पानि बेजाय महऽकैत है। साधू जन चलैत घुमैत रहथ, तबऽहो बेदाग रहैत छथ, कौनो दाग नऽ लगैछैन्ह।

चउठ बात।

एक दीन जाड़ा के दीन मेँ कौनो बड़ा आदिमी के घर आगि लगऽलैन्ह। सभ चीज बतुस जर जर राख भै गेलैन्ह। ऊ बहऽरा खड़ा हाथ मलैत रहथ, कि एतऽना मेँ एक गरीब परोसिया जाड़ा के मारल, थर थर कँपैत घर से निकस आएल, और हाथ सेदेँ लागल तब ऊ धनऽवाला कहलऽथिन्ह; वाह जि वाह, केकऽरो घर जरै केहू तापै॥

पाँचम बात।

बान्हल लकड़ी, आउर खूलल लकड़ी।

एक गिरहस्त के लरिका अपना में बहुत लरैत झगरैत रहथ; बात सभ से बड़ा समझौलक परन्तु केहू कुछु नऽ मनलकैक। तब गिरहस्त अपना जी में कहलक कि, अब हम हिन्हका कुछु कऽ कऽ देखाएब, तब आही जे बुझतन्ह। एक दीन ऊ अपना बेटा के बोलौलक, आउर कहलकैक जे, थोरे लकरी हमरा आगे ले आवऽ। ऊ सभ लकरी के ऊ गिरहस्त एक रस्सी से कस के बान्हलक। फेर सभ से कहलकैक जे रस्सी जन खोलऽ आउर लकरी सभ के तूर डालऽ। सभ केउ मिल परल परन्तु कुछु नऽ भेलैक। फेर गिरहस्त खोल कऽ एक एक गो लकरी हुन्ह के देलकैक, जेकरा के ऊ सभ झटपट तूर डाललक। तब उन्हकर बाप कहलकैक जे, ए बेटा जे तौं बान्हल लकरी नियर अपना में मिलल रहबऽ, तऽ सभ दुसमन के दाँत खट्टा होअत; आउर अब खुल गेलऽ; तऽ बूझऽ जे बिगर गेलऽ। खुलऽ से बिगरल।

छठम बात।

ऊँड़ाड़ सभ के आउर भेंड़ा सभ के मेल।

एक बेर ऊँड़ाड़ सभ भेंड़ा सभ से कह भेजलकैक जे, आवऽ, हम तौं अपना में मिलाप कर लीज। किअक अपना में लरब, आउर एक दोसरा के लेहू के पियासल रहब। ई पाजी कुत्ता सभ लराइ के जर है। एहिमा सदाय भूक भूक कऽ हमरा भड़कवैत है, आउर हमरा तोहरा से लरवैत है। एकरा के सभ हमरा पास भेज दऽ। फेर कहाँ झगरा है। हमरा आउर तोहरा में सदाय पियार आउर मिलाप रहत। तब एको तोहर बार टेढ़ नऽ होअत। गँवार भेंड़ा ऊ नटखट ऊँड़ाड़ सभ के बात मान लेलक, आउर कुत्ता सभ के ऊँड़ाड़ के पास भेज देलकैक। पहिलें तऽ ऊँड़ाड़ सभ कुत्ता सभ के खा गेल, फेर भेंड़ा सभ के पीछे आय के उपाय कैलक, आउर थोरन्ही दीन में सभ भेंड़ा के खा गेल॥ साँच है, बैरी सदाय धोखा देत है; ऊ बड़ गँवार है जे बैरी के साँच कऽ बुझैच॥

सातम बात।

बाघ आउर ऊँड़ाड़ आउर चीता।

एक बेर बाघ आउर ऊँड़ाड़ आउर चीता अपना में ई ठहरौलक जे, हम सभ केउ मिलऽ कऽ सिकार मारू। फेर अपना में बाँट लेब। ई ठान कऽ जङ्गल में कूदे फाने लागल, आउर जब एक बड़का ठो हरीन करिया मारलक, तब बाघ बाअल के आवक..

एकऽरा के बाँट लीज, आउर झट ओकऽरा तीन टुकऽरा कर देलैक, आउर चिचिया कऽ बाजल जे, पहिल टुकऽरा हमऽही लेब, किअक हम जङ्गल के राजा छी, आउर दोसऽरो हमऽहीं लेब, किअक हम एकऽरा के मारे मैं बड़ुत दौर धूप कैले छी; आउर तेसर टुकऽरा ई भेल है, देखऽ तऽ केकर मुँह परैत है जे हमऽरा आगाँ से उठा ले जाएत। ई सुन कऽ चीता आउर ऊँड़ाड़ लँगऽरी दबा कऽ भाग गेल, आउर बाघ हरीन के एकऽसरे घट कर गेले। ई कहावत साँच है, जेकर लाठी तेकऽरे * भैँस ॥

आठम बात।

माँटी आउर पीतर के घैला के बातऽचीत।

एक बेर नदी बढ़ल, तऽ एक पीतर के घैला, आउर एक माँटी के घैला बह चलल। तब पीतर के घैला माँटी के घैला से कहलऽकैक जे, हमऽरा सङ्गे लागल चलऽ, तऽ हम तोहऽरा बचा लेबौ। माँटी के घैला बाजल जे, ई बात आहाँ बड़ुत नीक कहऽली, हम आहाँ के भला मानब आउर सहाय गून गाएब; परन्तु साँच पूछी, तऽ हमऽरा ई डर है, जे कहईं पानि के हिलोरा के धक्का से आहाँ के लग नऽ जा रही; किअक कि जब आहाँ से दूरे रहब, तब ऐसेही हिलैत झुलैत कहीं तीर पर जा लागब, परन्तु जब आहाँ से भैँट भेल, आउर कहईं धोखा से टकर लग जाएत, तब हमरो पेट फाट जाएत। साँच है बड़ऽका सभ से भरोसा रक्खी, परन्तु लगे नऽ जाई ॥

नौवाँ बात।

एक मुनऽसी बजार मैं बैसल चिट्ठी लिखैत रहथ। एक बिदेसी आएल, आउर बाजल जे, मुनऽसी जी, की लिखैत छी। मुनऽसी जी जवाब देलऽथिन्ह जे, भैया चिट्ठी लिखैत छी। तब ऊ कहलऽकैन्ह जे, हमऽरो सलाम लिख दीज। मुनऽसी जी कहलऽथिन्ह जे नऽ जी, अरऽजी लिखैत छी। तब ऊ कहलऽकैन्ह जे, हमऽरो सही कर दीज। मुनऽसी जी अगुता कऽ बजलऽथिन्ह जे, तमस्सुक लिखैत छी। तब ऊ कहलऽकैन्ह जे, हमऽरो गोवाही लिख दीज। मुनऽसी जी सोचऽलन्ह जे, ई तऽ केहू अनोख ढङ्ग के आदिमी देखार † दैत है। पुछलऽथिन्ह जे, तोहर नाम की छौ। तब ऊ हँसल, आउर बाजल जे, हमर नाम है मानऽ नऽ मानऽ, हम तोहर मैहऽमान छी ॥

---

* Emphatic for तेकर.

† First verbal Noun of the potential passive.

दसम बात ।

एक बड़॰का लोक के घर मेँ रात क॰ आगि लग॰लैन्ह। ऊ त॰ अपन बाल बच्चा के ले क॰ निकस भग॰लन्ह। नोकर से ऊकुम देलन्ह, जे, चीज बतुस निकास॰। एत॰ना मेँ आगि बऊत बढ़ गेल; सौँसे घर धुआँ धुआँ हो गेल। नोकर बाजल जे, हम की की निकासू, तब ऊ बड़॰का आदिमी सुसुआए लग॰लन्ह, आउर कह॰लन्ह जे, बाबा, मकान मेँ आगि लागे, तब ओ निक॰से से लाभ है॥

इगार॰हम बात।
गँवार गोआरिनि ।

एगो गँवार * गोआरिनि माथा पर कह॰तरी रख॰ले जाइत रहे। जाइत जाइत ओक॰रा मन मेँ ई उमङ्ग उठ॰ले जे, ई दही के बेँचब, आउर ढेबुआ से आम मोल लेब; कुछु आम हम॰रा जोरे है, सभ मिला क॰ तीन से से कुछु बढ़ जाएत। एहि मेँ कुछु सड़ जाएत; परन्तु, हँ, अढ़ाई से त॰ बचत। आउर ओहि मेँ से जे बचत नीक दाम होएत, त॰ दिवारी मेँ एक हरिअर सारी लेब। हँ, हँ, हरिअर सारी हम॰रा मुँह पर नीक खुलत। आउर बस, हम त॰ हरिअरे सारी लेब; आउर ओक॰रा पहिर क॰ मेला जाएब; आउर खूब ऐँठ अँठ क॰ अप॰ना गह॰ना कप॰ड़ा के झमक आउर मुँह के चमक दमक देखाएब; आउर चलैत चलैत मेँ से से बेर ऐँठब। एहि सोच बिचार मेँ ऊ गँवार गोआरिनि जे कुछु चमक ठमक क॰ ढेढ़ चाल चलल, त॰ दही के कह॰तरी ओक॰रा माथा से गिर क॰ हक॰रा हक॰री हो गेलैक, आउर सभ बनल बनाओल घर बिगर गेलैक॥

बार॰हम बात।
चिल्होर आउर कौआ।

एक चिल्होर के लोल मेँ घोँघा रहैक। केत॰नो भुइँआँ मेँ पटक पटक फोर॰लक, परन्तु घोँघा न॰ फुट॰लैक। तब एक कौआ ई उपाय बतौल॰कैक जे, ई घोँघा के लोल मेँ ले क॰ बऊत ऊँच तक उड़ जाह, आउर उहाँ से गिरा द॰, तब घोँघा फट जाएत। चिल्होर कह॰लक जे ई बऊत नीक बात है, आउर घोँघा के ले क॰ उड़ल, आउर बऊत उपर जा क॰ छाड़ देलक। जौँ घोँघा भुइआँ मेँ गिरल, त॰ फूट फाट गेल, आउर कौआ ओकर गूदा चाक लेलक। थोरा बेर मेँ चिल्होर नीचा उत॰रल, तब छिलुका छाड़ क॰ आउर कुछु न॰ पौलक॥

---

* Fem. of गमार.

तेर॰हम बात।

खट्टा अँगूर।

एक खिखिर कौनो फुल॰वारी मेँ जा पहुँचल; देख॰लक जे अँगूर सभ के ऐसन गुच्छ पाकल टाटी मेँ लट॰कल है, कि ओकरा से रस चू रहल है, आउर कौनो रख॰वारो न॰ है। ई देख क॰ ओक॰रा मुँह मेँ पानि भर ऐलैक। ऊ बहुत तरहेँ उछ॰लल कूदल परन्तु अँगूर के गुच्छा तक न॰ पहुँच सक॰लैक। जब कौनो उपाय से दाव न॰ लग॰लैक, तब एना बड़॰बराता उहाँ से चलल, जे खट्टा अँगूर के खाओ॥

चौद॰हम बात।

रसाइनी।

एक रसाइनी कौनो आदिमी से कहल॰कैक जे, जोँ तोँ कुछु चानी हम॰रा पास ले आ॰, तोँ हम एक ऐसन जड़ी मिलाएब जे तुरन्त ही ऊ चानी के सोना हो जाएत। ऊ सोझिया सुधा आदिमी ओक॰रा पर॰तार मेँ आ गेल, आउर कहइँ से दुख सुख सह क॰ दू से रपैया के चानी ऊ रसाइनी के आन क॰ देल॰कैन्ह। रसाइनी ओही* रात क॰ अप्पन बिछौना उठा क॰ कहइँ चल गेल। तब ऊ बेचारा बिपत के मारल ओही ठग रसाइनी के खोज मेँ दौर धुप करे लागल, जङ्गल जङ्गल खोज मारलक, परन्तु ओई रसाइनी के पता कहइँ न॰ लग॰लैक। ओक॰रा एह तरह के घब॰राएल देख क॰, एक आदिमी कहल॰कैक जे, तोह॰रा से ई चूक भेलौ, कि ओह ठग अथीथ के फाँस मेँ फन्स गेल॰। परन्तु पछ॰तौला से आउर ओक॰रा खोज मेँ दौर धूप कैला से कुछु न॰ होतौ। एह बात पर हम एक बात तोह॰रा कहैछी, जे सदाय इआद रक्खे के चाही॥

पनर॰हम बात।

एक चिरइँ कौनो गिर॰हस्त के गाछी मेँ जा क॰ काँच पाकल फल सभ के सभ काट जाइत छल, त॰ गिर॰हस्त सभ दिना ओक॰रा खोज मेँ रहे। एक दीन अँगूर के टाटी पर जाल लगा क॰ ओक॰रा धैलक, आउर मारे के चह॰लक। चिरइँ गिर॰हस्त से कहल॰कैक जे, जोँ तोँ हम॰रा छाड़ दह, तोँ हम एहि भलाइ के बद॰ला तोह॰रा कै बात बता देबौ, कि जे सँ तोह॰रा बड़ लाभ होतै। गिर॰हस्त कहल॰कैक जे, पहिले बता दे त॰ हम तोह॰रा के छाड़ देबौक। चिरइँ ओक॰रा तीन बात कहल॰कैक, एक त॰ ई जे, बैरी अब अपन्ना बस मेँ आ जाए, त॰ छाड़े के न॰ चाही, दोसर जे बात ध्यान मेँ न॰ आवे, ओक॰रा न॰ माने के चाही

* Emphatic for ओह.

तेसर गेल चीज के लेल पछʼतावे के नं० चाही। चौथ एक त० आउर है। अब तों हमʼरा के छाड़ देब० त० हम कहबौ। किसान ई बात सभ क सुन क० जेना कहʼले रहैक तेसʼने कैलक, आउर ऊ चिरईं के छाड़ देलक। चिरईं भीत पर बैस क० कहलʼकैक जे, हमʼरा पेट मैं सुबगी के अण्डा से अः नमʼहर एक मोती रहल है, जौं तों हमʼरा नं० छाड़ित० आउर मारित०, तौं ऊ मोती तोहʼरा हाथ लगैत। गिरʼहस्त पछʼतावे लागल। ऊ कहलʼकैक जे, रे बुरʼबक तों हमर तीनो बात के अखʼनी भूल गेले; किअक कि हम तोहर बैरी छी, अब धैले रहे, त० छाड़ʼले किअक; आउर सुबगी के बराबर त० हमʼहीं नं० छी, फेर सुबगी के अण्डा से नमʼहर मोती हमʼरा पेट मैं कैसे आ सकैत है। परन्तु तों एह बात पर भरोसा कैल०, आउर अब हम तोहʼरा हाथ से निकस गेली, तब पछʼतौला से की हो सकैत है। एई से ईहे* फल निकʼसैत है, कि पहिले से सभ काम बहुत सोच बिचार क० करे के चाही, आउर अब कौनो काम बिगर जाए, त० फेर पछʼतावे के नं० चाही॥

सोरʼहम बात।

कौनो धनिक के दू बेटा रहैन्ह। जब ऊन्हʼकर बाप मर गेलैन्ह, तब दूनो भाइ ऊन्हʼकर धन अपʼना मैं बाँट लेलन्ह। बड़ʼका भाइ अप्पन रुपैया आउर ढेबुआ सुख चैन आउर खेल तमास: मैं उड़ा देलन्ह आउर छोटʼका भाइ बड़ जतन से बनिज बेपार करे लगʼलन्ह। एक दीन बड़ʼका भाइ छोटʼका भाइ के चोरʼहʼना दे क० कहलʼथिन्ह जे, ए भाइ, दीन भर अनाज किअक तौलैत रहैत छ०; हमʼरा सङ्गे रह०, आ पीअ, चैन कर०। बहुत दीन के पाछाँ, जब छोटʼका भाइ लोभाइ देनाइ से बहुत रुपैया एकट्ठा कैलक, तब ओ बड़ʼका भाइ, जे राग रङ्ग खेल तमासा मैं अप्पन सभ धन उड़ा पड़ा क० भिखार हो गेल रहे, ओकʼरा डेओढ़ी मैं आ क० कहे लगʼलैक जे, ए भैया, हम तोहʼरा पहिले ठट्ठा मैं ओरौले रही। परन्तु जौं हम तोहʼरा नाहित बनिज बेपार करʼती, आउर अनाज तौलʼती, तौं आज पा भर अनाज एक्के ओक्के से माँग क० नं० खैती। साँच है; आसʼकत ऐसʼने कीरा है, जे धन के मूरा कर देत है।

सतʼरहम बात।

लालʼची कुत्ता।

कौनो कुत्ता नदी के तीर पर एक हाड़ पौलक, आउर मुँह मैं लेलक। जबʼहीं करʼआहीं ओकर पानि मैं देखʼलक तबʼहीं समुझʼलक जे दोसर हाड़ है। मारे लालच के मुँह खोलʼलक, के ओकʼरो के पानि से निकास ली। नं० ऊ हाड़ जे मुँह मैं रहैक सेहो गेरा देलक। साँच है, लालच से माँछी दूध पर बैसल, पाँख लपʼटा गेलैक दूनो हाथ मल मल क० माँथ पीटे लागल, जे लालच बड़ बलाइ होइत है।

* Emphatic for ई.

APPENDIX II.

NOTE ON THE USE OF THE VARIOUS VERBAL TERMINATIONS.

NOTHING is more perplexing to the foreigner than the multiplicity of forms which occur for each person in the verbal conjugations. This multiplicity is partly due, no doubt, to local and personal circumstances, an inhabitant of one place using one set of forms, and an inhabitant of another, another; still at the same time it is not correct to say that all these forms are exactly synonymous, for frequently one person will be found using all the forms given in this Grammar, but each with a slightly different shade of meaning. Unfortunately, however, here again local circumstances come in, and an inhabitant of one place will be found using a form with a different shade of meaning from that used in another place. This is due to the want of a literature, which would fix each verbal form in its proper and exact shade of meaning. The Maithilí dialect (which is situated immediately to the east of that of Muzaffarpúr) fortunately has a fairly copious literature, and hence it uses all its verbal forms according to strict rule. Such is not the case with regard to Muzaffarpúr; and hence in the present state of the language, and of our knowledge of it, it is impossible to give more than a general guide as to the customary idiom of one tract.

The following facts have been kindly supplied to the writer by T. Norman, Esq., Collector of Muzaffarpúr, and deal only with the idiom of the tract of country immediately surrounding the head-quarters of the district.

When the object of the verb, direct or remote, or the predicate, is the second personal pronoun, or is the person addressed, and he is considered as the equal of the speaker, the termination अउ *aü* (pronounced ŏ-ŏ) is used. Thus तोहरा के के मारलकउ *tŏh'rá ke ke máral'kaü*, which may be translated, 'my friend, who has beaten you?'

Under similar circumstances when he is considered inferior to the speaker, the termination अौ *au* (pronounced like 'ow' in 'how') is used. Thus तोहरा गाड़ी मेँ की माल हौ *tŏh'rá gáṛí mē kí mál hau*, which may be translated, 'my humble friend, what goods are in your cart?

When the object of the verb, direct or remote, or the predicate, is in the third person and is mentioned with respect, the termination ऐन्ह *ainh* is used. Thus ऊ महाराज के पेड़ देबैन्ह *ú mahárāj ke peṛ dĕbainh*, which may be translated 'that gentleman will give a plant to the respected mahárájá.' Again महाराज के कुत्ता के के मारलकैन्ह *mahárāj kĕ kuttá ke ke máral'kainh*, —who has beaten the respected mahárájá's dog?

Under similar circumstances when he is inferior to the speaker, the termination ऐ *ai* is used. Thus ओकरा के के मारलकै *ŏk'rá ke ke máral'kai*, which may be translated, 'who has beaten that humble person, in whom I take an interest?'

In addition to the above, the warning given in § 35, that in colloquial Muzaffarpúrí the verb does *not* agree with its subject in number, must be borne in mind. In other words, it is that a singular subject continually governs a plural verb, and *vice versâ*.

Reg. No. 11531J—510—1-9-84.

SEVEN

GRAMMARS

OF THE DIALECTS AND SUBDIALECTS OF THE

BIHÁRÍ LANGUAGE.

SPOKEN IN THE PROVINCE OF BIHÁR, IN THE EASTERN PORTION OF THE NORTH-WESTERN PROVINCES, AND IN THE NORTHERN PORTION OF THE CENTRAL PROVINCES.

PART V.

SOUTH MAITHILÍ DIALECT

OF SOUTH DAṚBHANGÁ, NORTH MUNGER, AND THE MADHEPÚRÁ SUBDIVISIŌN OF BHAGALPÚR.

Compiled under orders of the Government of Bengal

By GEORGE A. GRIERSON, B.C.S.,

JOINT-MAGISTRATE OF PATNA,

CALCUTTA:

PRINTED AT THE BENGAL SECRETARIAT PRESS.

1885.

CONTENTS.

INTRODUCTION.

§ 1. The following grammar treats of the South Maithilí dialect, spoken in South Darbhangá, North Munger, and the Madhepúrá subdivision of Bhagalpúr. This dialect is founded on the much more archaic North Maithilí dialect spoken in North Darbhangá and the Supaul subdivision of Bhagalpúr. The people who speak it dwell along the north bank of the river Ganges, and the intercourse with foreigners thereby produced has tended to phonetically develop their language into a more convenient and flexible form than that of the somewhat cumbrous Northern Maithilí. A grammar and reading-book of Northern Maithilí has been published by the Asiatic Society of Bengal.* I have much pleasure in recording my thanks to Maul'wí Ibn-i-Husain, Head Master, Muhammadan Academy, Tájpur, who has given me valuable information regarding the dialect of South Darbhangá.

§ 2. The alphabet and rules for spelling will be found in the General Introduction to this series of grammars, and the remarks therein found are not repeated here.

---

* Introduction to the Maithilí Language of North Bihár. By G. A. Grierson.

	Rs.	A.	P.
Part I, Grammar (extra number, J. A. S. B., 1880)	2	0	0
Part II, Chrestomathy and Vocabulary (extra number, J. A. S. B., 1882)	4	0	0

DIVISION I.

DECLENSION.

CHAPTER I.

NOUNS.

§ 3. For general remarks, see the General Introduction, § 38 and ff.

The following are the post-positions used in declining the noun in this dialect :—

		Power.
Nom.	*Wanting.*	
Acc.	*Wanting* or के *ke*, कैँ *kẽ*, कै *kai*, or कैँ *kaĩ*.	
Instr.	से *se*, सेँ *sẽ*, सै *sai*, सैँ *saĩ*, or सोँ *sõ*.	'By.'
Dat.	के *ke*, केँ *kẽ*, कै *kai*, or कैँ *kaĩ*.	'To.'
	ले *le* or लेल *lel*.	'For.'
Abl.	से *se*, सेँ *sẽ*, सै *sai*, सैँ *saĩ*, or सोँ *sõ*.	'From.'
Gen.	क *k*, के *kĕ*, or केर *ker*.	'Of.'
Loc.	मेँ *mẽ* or मोँ *mõ*.	'In.'
Voc.	*Wanting.*	

All these post-positions will only be used in one example, that of घोरा *ghoṛá*, 'a horse ;' but they can all be used with all nouns.

. Except that for the genitive, they can be used with all pronouns. In the genitive singular many pronouns do not take these post-positions, but have other forms subject to special rules.

The plural is the same as the singular.

The following are examples of declension.

§ 4. (a) Masculine Tadbhavas in आ *á*.

Example of the declension of a *tadbhava** masculine noun in आ *á*:–

घोरा *ghorá*, 'a horse.'

Short form,	Weak, घोर *ghor*.	Long form,* घोरवा *ghŏr'wá*.
	Strong, घोरा *ghorá*.	Redundant form,† घोरौवा *ghŏrauwá*.

Singular.

Nom.	घोरा [1] *ghorá*,	'a horse.'
Acc.	घोरा *ghorá* or घोरा के *ghorá ke*, कँ *kẽ*, कै *kai*, or कैँ *kaĩ*,	'a horse.'
Instr.	घोरा से *ghorá se*, सँ *sẽ*, सै *sai*, सैँ *saĩ*, or सोँ *sõ*,	'by a horse.'
Dat.	घोरा के *ghorá ke*, कँ *kẽ*, कै *kai*, or कैँ *kaĩ*,	'to a horse.'
	घोरा ले *ghorá le* or लेल *lel*,	'for a horse.'
Abl.	घोरा से, *ghorá se*, सँ *sẽ*, सै *sai*, सैँ *saĩ*, or सोँ *sõ*,	'from a horse.'
Gen.	घोरक *ghorak*, घोरा के [2] *ghorá kĕ*, or घोरा केर *ghorá ker*,	'of a horse.'
Loc.	घोरा मेँ *ghorá mẽ* or मोँ *mõ*,	'in a horse.'
Voc.	ए घोरा *e ghorá !*	'O horse!'

[1] Or घोर *ghor*, घोरवा *ghŏr'wá*, or घोरौवा *ghŏrauwá*, and so throughout.

[2] The genitival affixes remain unchanged before all genders and cases.

Plural.

The plural is the same as the singular.

---

* See General Introduction, § 12.

† See General Introduction, §§ 12, 38, and ff.

§ 5. (b) Masculine Nouns ending in Silent Consonants.

Example of the declension of a masculine noun ending in a silent consonant:—

घौर *ghaur*, 'a house.'

Short form, घौर *ghaur*. Long form,* घौरवा *ghăūr'wá*. Redundant form,* घौरौवा *ghăūrauwá*.

Singular and Plural.

Nom.	घौर[1] *ghaur*,	'a house.'
Acc.	घौर, घौर कें *aur*, *ghaur kẽ*,	'a house.'
Instr.	घौरें *ghaurẽ*, घौर सँ *ghaur sẽ*,	'by a house.'
Dat.	घौर ले *ghaur le*,	'for a house.'
Abl.	घौर सँ *ghaur sẽ*,	'from a house.'
Gen.	घौरक *ghaurak*, घौर के *ghaur kĕ*,	'of a house.'
Loc.	घौरे *ghaure*, घौर मेँ *ghaur mẽ*,	'in a house.'
Voc.	ए घौर *e ghaur !*	'O house !'

[1] Or घौरवा *ghăūr'wá*, घौरौवा *ghăūrauwá*, and so throughout.

§ 6. It is not necessary to decline further any nouns in full, as the above examples suffice. All nouns ending in vowels are declined like घोरा *ghorá*, and all those ending in silent consonants like घौर *ghaur*. The final syllables of all long and redundant forms may optionally be nasalised by the addition of *anunásik :* thus घोरवा *ghŏr'wá* or घोरवाँ *ghŏr'wá̃ ;* घौरौवा *ghăūrauwá* or घौरौवाँ *ghăūrauwá̃ ;* मलिया *maliyá* or मलियाँ *maliyá̃*.

Note, however, that—

(1) Occasionally in the case of masculine nouns ending in a silent consonant we find an instrumental in ऐं *ẽ* and a locative in ए *e :* thus हम बलेँ ले जाएब *ham balẽ le jáĕb*, 'I shall take away by force,' where बलेँ *balẽ* is the instrumental of बल

* See General Introduction, §§ 12, 38, and ff.

bal, 'force;' घाटे *ghâṭe*, 'at a landing stage,' locative of घाट *ghâṭ*, 'a landing stage:' so also घौरे घौरे *ghaure ghaure*, 'in every house,' 'from house to house.'

(2) All nouns ending in a long vowel shorten it before the genitival termination क *k*: thus घोरक *ghorak* from घोरा *ghorá*.

(3) Certain verbal nouns ending in ल *l* have an oblique form in ला *lá*: thus देखल *dekhal*, abl. देखला से *dĕkh'lá se*, 'from seeing;' also verbal nouns in the form of the root have an oblique form in अ *a*, ए *ĕ*, or ऐ *aĭ*: thus देख *dekh*, dat. देखअ के *dekha ke*, देखे के *dekhĕ ke*, or देखै के *dekhaĭ ke*, 'for seeing.' Full particulars concerning these nouns will be found in § 111.

An example of each of the more common forms of nouns follows:—

§ 7. (c) Masculine Tatsamas* in आ *á*.

राजा *rájá*, 'a king.'

Short form, राजा *rájá*. Long form,* रजवा *raj'wá*. Redundant form,* रजौवा *rajauwá*.

Gen. sing. राजक *rájak*, राजा के *rájá kĕ*, &c.

§ 8. (d) Masculine Nouns in ई *í*.

माली *málí*, 'a gardener.'

Short form, माली *málí*. Long form,* मलिया *maliyá*. Redundant form,* मलियवा *maliyawá* or मलौवा *malwá*.

Gen. sing. मालिक *málik*, माली के *málí kĕ*, &c.

---

* See General Introduction, §§ 12, 38, and ff., 34 and 36.

§ 9. (e) Masculine Nouns in ऊ *ú*.

नाऊ *náú*, 'a barber.'*

Short form, नाऊ *náú*. Long form,† नउआ *naüá* or नौआ *nauá*. Redundant form,† नउअवा *naüawá* or नौअवा *nauawá*.

Gen. sing. नाउक *náük*, नाऊ के *náú kĕ*, &c.

§ 10. (f) Feminine Nouns in ई *í* and इ *i*.

पोथी *pothí*, 'a book.'

Short form, पोथी *pothí*. Long form,† पोथिया *pŏthiyá*. Redundant form,† पोथियवा *pŏthiyawá* or पोथीवा *pothíwá*.

Gen. sing. पोथिक *pothik*, पोथी के *pothí kĕ*, &c.

राति *ráti* 'night.'

Short form, राति *ráti*. Long form,† रतिया *ratiyá*. Redundant form,† रतियवा *ratiyawá* or रतीवा *ratíwá*.

Gen. sing. रातिक *rátik*, राति के *ráti kĕ*, &c.

§ 11. (g) Feminine Nouns ending in a Silent Consonant.

बात *bát*, 'a word.'

Short form, बात *bát*. Long form,† बतिया *batiyá*. Redundant form,† बतियवा *batiyawá* or बतीवा *batíwa*.

Gen. sing. बातक *bátak*, बात के *bát kĕ*, &c.

---

* Kellogg in his Hindí Grammar incorrectly gives आँसू *ású* as an example of a feminine noun in ऊ *ú*: it is masculine. आँसू *ású* is not used in Bihárí, लोर *lor* being the word for 'a tear.'

† See General Introduction, §§ 12, 38, and ff., 34 and 36.

§ 12. Periphrastic Plural.

With reference to the statement that the plural forms are the same as the singular, it must be noted that every noun can also form a periphrastic plural by the addition, either before or after, of a word signifying plurality, such as सभ *sabh*, 'all :' thus, सभ घोरा *sabh ghora*, or घोरा सभ *ghora sabh*, 'horses.' In the case of rational beings the word लोग *log*, 'people,' may be used, but only *after* the word which becomes plural; thus, माली लोग *málí log*, 'gardeners,' and not लोग माली *log málí*.

§ 13. Genitival Affixes.

The following examples have been specially designed to exhibit the use of the genitival affixes :--

1.	ई राजा के (or केर) मन्दिर छिकै. *I rájá kĕ* (or *ker*) *mandir chhikai.*	'This is the king's temple.'
2.	हमें कन्स के (or कन्सक) नौरी छिकों. *Hamĕ Kans kĕ* (or *kansak*) *nauri chhikŏ.*	'I am the maid-servant of King Kans.'
3.	मधमाखि के (or केर) झुण्ड उर गेलै, *Madh'mákhi kĕ* (or *ker*) *jhuṇḍ ur gĕlai,* or मधुमाछिक झुण्ड उड़ गेलै. *Madhumáchhik jhuṇḍ uṛ gĕlai.*	'A swarm of bees flew away.'
4.	छली के मारे मों दोख नहीं. *Chhalí kĕ márĕ mŏ dokh nahí.* कपटी के मारःबक कौनो दोख नै. *Kap'ṭi kĕ már'bak kauno dokh nai.*	'There is no sin in slaying a deceiver.'
5.	मथुरा के नारी सभ कनैत चलल गेली. *Mathurá kĕ nárí sabh kanait chalal geli.*	'The women of Mathurá departed weeping.'

6.	बहुत तरह के बात सुनल गेल. *Bahut tarah kĕ bát sunal gel.*	'Matters of many kinds were heard.'
7.	स्फटिक के चारि फाटक टूटि गेलै. *Sphaṭik kĕ chári pháṭak ṭúṭi gĕlai.*	'Four gates of crystal broke.'
8.	देस देस के राजा सभ ऐला. *Des des kĕ rájá sabh ailá.*	'Kings of all countries came.'
9.	ऊ सभ माली के बेटा छिका. *Ú sabh máli kĕ beṭá chhiká.*	'They are the sons of the gardener.'
10.	हमें राजा के गाँव में ऐलौं. *Hamẽ rájá kĕ gãw mẽ aĩlaũ.*	'I came into the king's villages.'
11.	पण्डितक घौर में बहुत तरह के पुस्तक छैन. *Paṇḍitak ghaur mẽ bahut tarah kĕ pustak chhain.*	'There are many books in paṇḍits' houses.'

CHAPTER II.

ADJECTIVES.

§ 14. Gender.

See General Introduction, § 42 and ff.

§ 15. Numeral Adjectives.

The cardinals are nearly the same as those in High Hindí. The following are the ones that present points of difference :—

1 = एक *ĕk.*
2 = दू *dú* or दोँ *dŏ̃.*
6 = छौ *chhau.*
11 = एगारह *ĕgárah.*
15 = पन॰रह *pan'rah* or पन्द॰रह [*pand'rah.*
16 = सोरह *sorah.*
21 = एकैस *ĕkais.*
31 = एक॰तिस *ĕk'tis.*
32 = बत्तिस *battis.*
33 = तेँतिस *tĕ̃tis.*
34 = चौँतिस *chaũtis.*
35 = पैँतिस *pãĩtis.*
36 = छत्तिस *chhattis.*
37 = सैँतिस *sãĩtis.*
38 = अर॰तिस *ar'tis.*
39 = उन॰तालिस *un'tális* or उन॰-[चालिस *un'chális.*
40 = चालिस *chális.*
41 = एक॰तालिस *ĕk'tális.*
42 = बेआलिस *bĕális.*
43 = तेँतालिस *tĕ̃tális.*
44 = चवालिस *chawális.*
45 = पैँतालिस *pãĩtális.*
46 = छियालिस *chhiyális.*
47 = सैँतालिस *sãĩtális.*
48 = अर॰तालिस *ar'tális.*
54 = चौवन *chauwan.*
64 = चौसठ *chȧusaṭh.*
66 = छियासठ *chhiyásaṭh.*
67 = सर॰सठ *sar'saṭh.*
74 = चौहत्तर *chauhattar.*
82 = बेआसी *bĕásí* or बेरासी [*bĕrásí.*
84 = चौरासी *chaŭrásí.*
86 = छियासी *chhiyásí.*
94 = चौरानबे *chaŭránawe.*
96 = छियानबे *chhiyánawe.*
100 = सै *sai.*

§ 16. Ordinals.

The ordinals up to 'sixth' are as follows :—

1*st* = पहिल *pahil* ; *obl.* पहिला *pahilá* or पहऽला *pah'lá.**
2*nd* = दोसर *dosar* ; *obl.* दोसऽरा *dos'rá.**
3*rd* = तेसर *tesar* ; *obl.* तेसऽरा *tĕs'rá.**
4*th* = चारिम *chárim* or चारम *cháram.*
5*th* = पाँचिम *pắchim* or पाँचम *pắcham.*
6*th* = छठम *chhaṭham.*

The ordinals above 'sixth' are all formed by adding म *m* to the cardinals : as दसम *dasam*, 'tenth ;' पचासम *pachásam*, 'fiftieth.'

§ 17. Fractional Numbers.

These are—

$\frac{1}{4}$ = पौ *pau* or पौआ *pauá.*
$\frac{1}{3}$ = तेखऽरी *tĕkh'rí* or तेसऽरी *tĕs'rí.*
$\frac{1}{2}$ = आध *ádh*, आधा *ádhá*, or आधे *ádhe.*
$\frac{3}{4}$ = पौन *paun.*
$-\frac{1}{4}$ = पौने *paune.*
$+\frac{1}{4}$ = सवा *sawá.*
$1\frac{1}{4}$ = सवैया *sawaiyá.*
$1\frac{1}{2}$ = डेढ़ *ḍeṛh*, डेढ़ा *ḍeṛhá*, or डेर *ḍer.*
$2\frac{1}{2}$ = अढ़ाइ *aṛháï*, अराइ *aráï*, or अढ़िया *aṛhiyá.*
$+\frac{1}{2}$ = साढ़े *sáṛhe* or सारेह *sárĕh.*

§ 18. Multiplicatives.

Multiplicatives, such as the English 'twice' and 'thrice,' are not found in this dialect. The Bihárí idiom is illustrated in such phrases as दू सते चौदह *dú sate chaudah*, 'two seven's, fourteen ;' छौ ती अठारह *chhau tí*

---

* The first three ordinals follow pronominal genitives in the formation of oblique forms. See *post*, § 34.

aṭhárah, 'six three's, eighteen,' which correspond to the English idioms 'seven times two' and 'three times six.' Numbers thus used are called multiplicatives, and differ in some respects from the cardinals. The following are the multiplicative numbers up to 10, including fractions :—

× 1, कँ *kă* or काँइ *kăi*.
× 1¼, समऽ *sama*, सवैये *sawaiye*.
× 1½, डेओढ़ा *ḍĕoṛhá*.
× 2, दून *dūn*, दूना *dúná*, दोबर *dobar*.
× 2½, ढाम *ḍhám*, अढ़ैया *aṛhaiyá*.
× 3, ती *tí*, तिया *tiyá*.
× 3½, हूँठा *hū̃ṭhá*.
× 4, चौका *chauká*, चौच *chauch*.
× 4½, धौँचा *dhaũchá*, ढोँचा *ḍhŏcha*.
× 5, पचे *pache*, पञ्जे *panje*.
× 5½, पहुँचा *pahuńchá*, पोँचा *pŏcha*.
× 6, छक *chhak*, छका *chhaká*, or छक्का *chhakká*.
× 6½, खोँचा *khŏchá*.
× 7, सते *sate*, सात *sát*.
× 7½, सतोँचा *satŏchá*.
× 8, आठे *áṭṭhe*, अट्ठा *aṭṭha*.
× 9, नमऽ *nama*, नवेँ *nawĕ*.
× 10, दहम *daham*, दहाँइ *dahăi*.

§ 19. Definite Cardinals.

These are as follows :—

दूओँ *dúŏ*, दुन्नोँ *dunnŏ*, 'the two,' 'both ;'
तीनोँ *tínŏ*, 'the three ;'
चारोँ *chárŏ*, 'the four ;' and so on,

adding ओँ *ŏ* to the numerals, after omitting a final short vowel. Example: पाँचो भाइ जौरे छथ *păchŏ bhái jaure chhath*, 'the five brothers are an undivided family.'

§ 20. Indefinite Cardinals.

The termination अन *an* added to the numbers 'one hundred,' 'one thousand,' and so on, always denotes an indefinite number of these aggregates. In this idiom सैकर *saikar* is always substituted for सै *sai*, 'one hundred.' Examples are सैकड़न पेड़ *saĭk'ran peṛ*, 'hundreds of trees;' हजारन *hajáran*, 'thousands;' लाखन *lákhan*, 'tens of thousands;' हजारन अदिमी मरलन *hajáran adimi mar'lan*, 'thousands of men died.'

§ 21. Collective Numerals.

These—viz. जोरा *jorá*, 'a pair,' गंडा *gaṇḍá*, 'a four'—are the same as in High Hindí, except सैकड़ा *saĭk'rá*, 'a hundred.'

CHAPTER III.

PRONOUNS.

§ 22. The following tables show the declensional forms of the principal pronouns and pronominal forms.

The declension of pronouns presents some important points of difference from that of nouns, which must be carefully noticed.

While nouns frequently remain unchanged before post-positions, pronouns, with few exceptions, change to some other form, called the *oblique* or *inflected base.*

The accusative singular of pronouns is, with one or two exceptions, never the same as the nominative. The only exception is किछु *kichhu*, 'anything,' 'something.' In circumstances corresponding to those in which the accusative of a noun takes the nominative form, the accusative of a pronoun takes the oblique form without any post-position.

The genitive forms of pronouns ending in र *r* and न *n* are also to be noticed. They have all oblique forms ending in रा *rá* or ना *ná*, for which see § 34.

Pronouns have the same form, whether referring to masculine or feminine nouns. With the exception of the pronouns of the second person, they all want the vocative case.

§ 23. Pronouns of the First Person and of the Second Person Non-Honorific.

These pronouns have each two forms—a shorter and a longer.

हम *ham*, 'I.'

Singular.

	Shorter form.	*Longer form.*
Nom.	*Wanting.*	हम *ham*, हमे *hame*, or हमेँ *hamẽ*.
Acc.	मोरा[1] *morá* or मोरा केँ *morá kẽ*.	हमरा[1] *ham'rá* or हमरा केँ *ham'rá kẽ*.
Instr.	मोरा सेँ *morá sẽ*.	हमरा सेँ *ham'rá sẽ*.
Dat.	मोरा लेल *morá lel*.	हमरा लेल *ham'rá lel*.
Abl.	मोरा सेँ *morá sẽ*.	हमरा सेँ *ham'rá sẽ*.
Gen.	मोर *mor*, मोरे *morĕ*, or मोरऽ *mora*.	हमर *hamar*, हमरे *ham'rĕ*, or हमरऽ *ham'ra*.
Loc.	मोरा मेँ *morá mẽ*.	हमरा मेँ *ham'rá mẽ*.
Voc.	*Wanting.*	*Wanting.*

[1] मोरो *moro* and हमरो *ham'ro* may be used for मोरा *morá* and हमरा *ham'rá* in an emphatic sense: thus हमरो दऽ *ham'ro da*, 'give to me also.' In poetry a shorter oblique form, मोहि *mŏhi*, instead of मोरा *morá*, is sometimes found.

Plural.

	Shorter form.	*Longer form.*
Nom.	हम[1] *ham* or हम[1] सभ[2] *ham sabh*	हमरा सभ[2] *ham'rá sabh*.
Acc.	हम सभ (केँ) *ham sabh* (*kẽ*).	हमरा सभ (केँ) *ham'rá sabh* (*kẽ*).
Instr.	हम सभ सेँ *ham sabh sẽ*.	हमरा सभ सेँ *ham'rá sabh sẽ*.
Dat.	हम सभ लेल *ham sabh lel*.	हमरा सभ लेल *ham'rá sabh lel*.
Abl.	हम सभ सेँ *ham sabh sẽ*.	हमरा सभ सेँ *ham'rá sabh sẽ*.
Gen.	हमर सभ *hamar sabh* or हम सभक *ham sabhak*, &c.	हमरा सभ के *ham'rá sabh kĕ*.
Loc.	हम सभ मेँ *ham sabh mẽ*.	हमरा सभ मेँ *ham'rá sabh mẽ*.
Voc.	*Wanting.*	*Wanting.*

[1] Or हमे *hame* or हमेँ *hamẽ*, and so throughout.

[2] Or सभी *sabhí* or लोग *log*, and so throughout.

तोँ *tõ* or तूँ *tú*, 'thou.'

Singular.

	Shorter form.	*Longer form.*
Nom.	*Wanting.*	तोँ *tõ*, तोँह *tõh*, or तोहेँ *tohẽ*.
Acc.	तोरा[1] *torá* or तोरा केँ *torá kẽ*.	तोहन्रा[1] or तोहन्रा केँ *tŏh'rá* or *tŏh'rá kẽ*.
Instr.	तोरा सेँ *torá sẽ*.	तोहन्रा सेँ *tŏh'rá sẽ*.
Dat.	तोरा लेल *torá lel*.	तोहन्रा लेल *tŏh'rá lel*.
Abl.	तोरा सेँ *torá sẽ*.	तोहन्रा सेँ *tŏh'rá sẽ*.
Gen.	तोर *tor*, तोरे *torĕ*, or तोरऽ *tora*.	तोहर *tohar*, तोहन्रे *tŏh'rĕ*, or तोहन्रऽ *tŏh'ra*.
Loc.	तोरा मेँ *torá mẽ*.	तोहन्रा मेँ *tŏh'rá mẽ*.
Voc.	*Wanting.*	ए तोँ *e tõ* or ए तोँह *e tõh*.

[1] तोरो *toro* and तोहन्रो *tŏh'ro* may be used for तोरा *torá* and तोहन्रा *tŏh'rá* in an emphatic sense: thus तोहन्रो देखैछी *tŏh'ro dĕkhaichhí*, 'I see you also.' In poetry, a shorter oblique form, तोहि *tŏhi* instead of तोरा *torá*, is sometimes found.

Plural.

	Shorter form.	*Longer form.*
Nom.	तोँ[1] सभ[2] *tõ sabh*, or तोँह *tõh* or तोहेँ *tohẽ*.	तोहन्रा सभ[2] *tŏh'rá sabh*.
Acc.	तोँ सभ (केँ) *tõ sabh (kẽ)*.	तोहन्रा सभ (केँ) *tŏh'rá sabh (kẽ)*.
Instr.	तोँ सभ सेँ *tõ sabh sẽ*.	तोहन्रा सभ सेँ *tŏhrá sabh sẽ*.
Dat.	तोँ सभ लेल *tõ sabh lel*.	तोहन्रा सभ लेल *tŏh'rá sabh lel*.
Abl.	तोँ सभ सेँ *tõ sabh sẽ*.	तोहन्रा सभ सेँ *tŏh'rá sabh sẽ*.
Gen.	तोहर सभ *tohar sabh* or तोँ सभक *tõ sabhak*, &c.	तोहन्रा सभ के *tŏh'rá sabh kĕ*.
Loc.	तोँ सभ मेँ *tõ sabh mẽ*.	तोहन्रा सभ मेँ *tŏh'rá sabh mẽ*.
Voc.	*Wanting.*	हे तोँह सभ *he tõh sabh*.

[1] Or तोँह *tõh* or तोहेँ *tohẽ*, and so throughout.

[2] Or सभी *sabhí* or लोग *log*, and so throughout.

§ 24. Pronoun of the Second Person Honorific and Reflexive Pronoun.

आइस *áïs*, अहाँ *ahã́*, or अप॰ने *ap'nĕ*, 'your honor.'

This pronoun is declined regularly like a substantive : thus—

आइस कँ *áïs kẽ*, अहाँ कँ *ahã́ kẽ*, or अप॰ने कँ *ap'nĕ kẽ*.
आइस सँ *áïs sẽ*, अहाँ सँ *ahã́ sẽ*, or अप॰ने सँ *ap'nĕ sẽ*, &c.

The nominative plural is आइस लोग *áïs log*, अहाँ लोग *ahã́ log*, or अप॰ने *ap'nĕ log*. Or सभ *sabh* may be used instead of लोग *log*.

आइस *áïs*, अप॰नैँ *ap'naĩ*, or अप॰ने *ap'nĕ*, 'self.'

This presents some irregularities, and is therefore declined in full.

	Singular.	*Plural.*
Nom.	आइस *áïs*, अप॰नैँ *ap'naĩ*, or अप॰ने *ap'nĕ*.	आइस सभ *áïs sabh*, अप॰नैँ सभ *ap'naĩ sabh*, or अप॰ने सभ *ap'nĕ sabh*.
Acc.	अप॰ना[1] (कँ) *ap'ná (kẽ)*.	अप॰ना[1] सभ (कँ) *ap'ná sabh (kẽ)*.
Instr.	अप॰ना सँ *ap'ná sẽ*.	अप॰ना सभ सँ *ap'na sabh sẽ*.
Dat.	अप॰ना लेल *ap'ná lel*.	अप॰ना सभ लेल *ap'ná sabh lel*.
Abl.	अप॰ना सँ *ap'ná sẽ*.	अप॰ना सभ सँ *ap'ná sabh sẽ*.
Gen.	अप्पन *appan*, आपन *ápan*, or अप॰ने *ap'nĕ*, अप॰नऽ *ap'na*.	आपुस के or केर *ápus kĕ* or *ker*.
Loc.	अप॰ना मेँ *ap'ná mẽ*.	आपुस मेँ *ápus mẽ*.

[1] Or आइस *áïs*, अप॰नैँ *ap'naĩ*, or अप॰ने *ap'nĕ*, and so throughout.

§ 25. Demonstrative Pronouns.

These are (1) the proximate demonstrative ई *í*, 'this,' and (2) the remote demonstrative ऊ *ú*, 'that.'

Like the personal pronouns, they have each two forms, a shorter and a longer.

ई *í*, 'this.'

Singular.

	Shorter form.	*Longer form.*
Nom.	इ *i*, ई *í*, ऐ *ai*, or इएँ *iĕ*.	*Wanting.*
Acc.	एहि (कँ) *ĕhi* (*kẽ*).	एक॰रा (कँ) *ĕk'rá* (*kẽ*).
Instr.	एहि सँ *ĕhi sẽ*.	एक॰रा सँ *ĕk'rá sẽ*.
Dat.	एहि लेल *ĕhi lel*.	एक॰रा लेल *ĕk'rá lel*.
Abl.	एहि सँ *ĕhi sẽ*.	एक॰रा सँ *ĕk'rá sẽ*.
Gen.	एहि के *ĕhi kĕ*.	एकर *ekar*, or एक॰रा के, केर *ĕk'rá kĕ, ker*.
Loc.	एहि मँ, *ĕhi mẽ*.	एक॰रा मँ *ĕk'rá mẽ*.

Plural.

	Shorter form.	*Longer form.*
Nom.	हिन्हि *hinhi*, हिनि *hini*, इन्ह *inh*, or इन *in*.	*Wanting.*
Acc.	इन्ह[1] (कँ) *inh* (*kẽ*).	इन्ह॰करा[3] (कँ) *inh'kará* (*kẽ*).
Instr.	इन्ह सँ *inh sẽ*.	इन्ह॰करा सँ *inh'kará sẽ*.
Dat.	इन्ह लेल *inh lel*.	इन्ह॰करा लेल *inh'kará lel*.
Abl.	इन्ह सँ *inh sẽ*.	इन्ह॰करा सँ *inh'kará sẽ*.
Gen.	इन्हक[2] *inhak* or इन्ह के, केर *inh kĕ, ker*.	इन्ह॰कर[4] *inh'kar* or इन्ह॰करा के, केर *inh'kará kĕ, ker*.
Loc.	इन्ह मँ *inh mẽ*.	इन्ह॰करा मँ, *inh'kará mẽ*.

[1] Or हिन्ह *hinh*, इन *in*, or हिन *hin*, and so throughout.

[2] Or हिन्हक *hinhak*, इनक *inak*, or हिनक *hinak*.

[3] Or हिन्ह॰करा *hinh'kará*, इन॰करा *in'kará*, हिन॰करा *hin'kara*, इन्ह॰केरा *inh'kĕrá*, हिन्ह॰केरा *hinh'kĕrá*, इन॰केरा *in'kĕrá*, हिन॰केरा *hin'kĕrá*, इन्ह॰का *inh'ká*, हिन्ह॰का *hinh'ká*, इन॰का *in'ká*, or हिन॰का *hin'ká*, and so throughout.

[4] Or हिन्ह॰कर *hinh'kar*, इन॰कर *in'kar*, or हिन॰कर *hin'kar*.

NOTE.—The plural of this pronoun is used in a singular honorific sense. To form the non-honorific plural, the word सभ *sabh* is added to any of the above forms: thus, nominative plural ई सभ *í sabh*, एक॰रा सभ *ĕk'rá sabh*, इन्ह सभ *inh sabh*, हिन्ह॰करा सभ *hinh'kará sabh*, and so on.

ऊ *u*, 'that.'

The close analogy between the declension of this pronoun and that of ई *í*, 'this,' will be manifest from the following paradigm:—

Singular.

	Shorter form.	*Longer form.*
Nom.	उ *u*, ऊ *ú*, औ *au*, or उआँ *uã*.	*Wanting.*
Acc.	ओहि (कँ) *ŏhi* (*kẽ*).	ओकऽरा (कँ) *ŏk'rá* (*kẽ*).
Instr.	ओहि सँ *ŏhi sẽ*.	ओकऽरा सँ *ŏk'rá sẽ*.
Dat.	ओहि लेल *ŏhi lel*.	ओकऽरा लेल *ŏk'rá lel*.
Abl.	ओहि सँ *ŏhi sẽ*.	ओकऽरा सँ *ŏk'rá sẽ*.
Gen.	ओहि के *ŏhi kĕ*.	ओकर *okar*, or ओकऽरा के, केर *ŏk'rá kĕ, ker*.
Loc.	ओहि मेँ *ŏhi mẽ*.	ओकऽरा मेँ *ŏk'rá mẽ*.

Plural.

	Shorter form.	*Longer form.*
Nom.	हुन्हि *hunhi*, हुनि *huni*, उन्ह *unh*, or उन *un*.	*Wanting.*
Acc.	उन्ह[1] (कँ) *unh* (*kẽ*).	उन्हऽकरा[3] (कँ) *unh'kará* (*kẽ*).
Instr.	उन्ह सँ *unh sẽ*.	उन्हऽकरा सँ *unh'kará sẽ*.
Dat.	उन्ह लेल *unh lel*.	उन्हऽकरा लेल *unh'kará lel*.
Abl.	उन्ह सँ *unh sẽ*.	उन्हऽकरा सँ *unh'kará sẽ*.
Gen.	उन्हक[2] *unhak* or उन्ह के, केर *unh kĕ, ker*.	उन्हऽकर[4] *unh'kar* or उन्हऽकरा के, केर *unh'kará kĕ, ker*.
Loc.	उन्ह मेँ *unh mẽ*.	उन्हऽकरा मेँ *unh'kará mẽ*.

[1] Or हुन्ह *hunh*, उन *un*, or हुन *hun*, and so throughout.

[2] Or हुन्हक *hunhak*, उनक *unak*, or हुनक *hunak*.

[3] Or हुन्हऽकरा *hunh'kará*, उनऽकरा *un'kará*, हुनऽकरा *hun'kará*, उन्हऽकेँरा *unh'kĕrá*, हुन्हऽकेँरा *hunh'kĕrá*, उनऽकेँरा *un'kĕrá*, हुनकेँरा *hun'kĕrá*, उन्हऽका *unh'ká*, हुन्हऽका *hunh'ká*, उनऽका *un'ká*, or हुनऽका *hun'ká*, and so throughout.

[4] Or हुन्हऽकर *hunh'kar*, उनऽकर *un'kar*, or हुनऽकर *hun'kar*.

NOTE.—The plural of this pronoun is used in a singular honorific sense. To form the non-honorific plural, the word सभ *sabh* is added to any of the above forms: thus, nominative plural ऊ सभ *ú sabh*, ओकरा सभ *ŏk'rá sabh*, उन्ह सभ *unh sabh*, हुन्हकरा सभ *hunh'kará sabh*, and so on.

NOTE.—In the above two demonstrative pronouns the shorter form may be used either adjectivally or substantivally, but the longer form can only be used as a substantive, and never as an adjective.

§ 26. Correlative Pronouns.

These are (1) the relative pronoun जे *je*, 'who;' (2) the correlative pronoun से *se*, 'that;' and (3) the interrogative pronoun के *ke*, 'who?'

The close analogy between their forms should be noted. Like the personal and demonstrative pronouns, they have each a shorter and a longer form.

It is not necessary to give their declension in full, as it is on exactly the same lines as that of the demonstrative pronouns. I shall therefore give only the nominative, genitive, and general oblique forms for each number.

Relative.

जे *je*, 'who.'

Singular.

	Shorter form.	*Longer form.*
Nom.	जे *je*.	*Wanting*.
Gen.	जेहि के *jĕhi kĕ*.	जेकर *jekar*.
Obl.	जेहि *jĕhi*.	जेकरा *jĕk'rá*.

Plural.

Nom.	जिन्हि *jinhi*, जिन्ह *jinh*, or जिन *jin*.	*Wanting*.
Gen.	जिन्हक *jinhak* or जिन्ह के *jinh kĕ*.	जिन्हकर *jinh'kar*.
Obl.	जिन्ह *jinh*.	जिन्हकरा *jinh'kará*.

Correlative.

से *se*, 'that.'

Singular.

	Shorter form.	*Longer form.*
Nom.	से *se.*	*Wanting.*
Gen.	तेहि के *tĕhi kĕ.*	तेकर *tekar.*
Obl.	तेहि *tĕhi.*	तेकऽरा *tĕk'rá.*

Plural.

Nom.	तिन्हि *tinhi*, तिन्ह *tinh*, or तिन *tin.*	*Wanting.*
Gen.	तिन्हक *tinhak* or तिन्ह के *tinh kĕ.*	तिन्हऽकर *tinh'kar.*
Obl.	तिन्ह *tinh.*	तिन्हऽकरा *tinh'kará.*

Interrogative.

के *ke*, 'who?'

Singular.

	Shorter form.	*Longer form.*
Nom.	के *ke.*	*Wanting.*
Gen.	केहि के *kĕhi kĕ.*	केकर *kekar.*
Obl.	केहि *kĕhi.*	केकऽरा *kĕk'rá.*

Plural.

Nom.	किन्हि *kinhi*, किन्ह *kinh*, or किन *kin.*	*Wanting.*
Gen.	किन्हक *kinhak* or किन्ह के *kinh kĕ.*	किन्हऽकर *kinh'kar.*
Obl.	किन्ह *kinh.*	किन्हऽकरा *kinh'kará.*

Other optional forms as in the demonstrative pronouns.

NOTE.—In the above correlative pronouns the shorter form may be used either adjectivally or substantivally, but the longer form can only be used as a substantive, and never as an adjective. As in the case of the demonstrative pronouns, the non-honorific plural is formed by adding सभ *sabh.*

§ 27. Interrogative Pronoun.

SUBSTANTIVAL.

की *ki*, 'what?'

This pronoun is really a neuter form of के *ke*, and can only refer to inanimate things. Its plural is the same as that of के *ke*.

Singular.

Nom. की *ki*.

Obl. कथी *kathi*, केथी *kěthi*, or काहे *káhě*, कहि *kahi*, किये *kiye*.

Declined regularly like a substantive. Its dative,—कथी ले *kathi le*, 'for that,' is used as an adverb, meaning 'why.'

§ 28. Indefinite Pronoun.

केऊ *kĕú*, 'anyone,' 'some one.'

This is declined throughout the singular and plural; but the plural is always used in a singular honorific sense.

Singular.

Nom. केऊ *kĕú*, कोइ *koï*, or कोय *koy*.

Obl. केकरो *kĕk'rŏ*, केकरौ *kĕk'raŭ*.

Declined regularly like a substantive, except the genitive, which is केकरो *kĕk'rŏ* or केकरौ *kĕk'raŭ*.

Plural.

Nom. Same as singular.

Obl. किनकरौ *kin'karaŭ* or किन्हकरौ *kinh'karaŭ*.

Declined regularly like a substantive, except the genitive, which is किनकरौ *kin'karaŭ* or किन्हकरौ *kinh'karaŭ*.

§ 29. किछु *kichhu*, 'anything,' 'something.'

Nom. किछु *kichhu*, कुछ *kuchh*, or कियुछ *kiyuchh*.
Obl. कथू *kathú*, किछु *kichhu*, कुछ *kuchh*, किछिओ *kichhiŏ*, or कथियो *kathiyŏ*.

Declined regularly like a substantive in the singular. The plural is wanting.

§ 30. The indefinite pronoun सभ *sabh* or सभी *sabhi*, 'all,' 'every one,' is declined regularly like a substantive. When plurality is to be emphasised, it has an oblique plural form सभनि *sabhani*: thus, सभ के *sabh kĕ*, 'of all,' *taken as a whole*; but सभनि के *sabhani kĕ*, 'of all,' *taken severally*.

§ 31. The indefinite pronouns जेकेउ *jekĕú*, 'whoever,' and जेकिछु *jekichhu*, 'whatever,' are compounds, and are declined regularly like their component parts: thus, acc. sing. जेह केकरो कैँ *jĕh kĕk'rŏ kẽ*, जेह किछु कैँ *jĕh kichhu kẽ*; instr. जेह केकरो सँ *jĕh kĕk'rŏ sẽ*, &c.

The indefinite pronominal adjective कै *kai*, कइ *kaï*, कैएक *kaiĕk* or कैक *kaik*, signifies 'several.' It is also used as an interrogative, meaning 'how many?'

§ 32. Derivative Pronominal Forms.

The following table gives the more usual pronominal adjectives and adverbs in a succinct form.

		Pronoun.	Manner.	
			Pron. Adj.	Pron. Adv.
Demonstrative ...	Proximate ...	ई *í*, 'this' ...	ऐसन *aisan*, एहन *ěhan*, 'of this kind.'	एना *ená*, 'thus.'
	Remote ...	ऊ *ú*, 'that' ...	वैसन *waisan*, औसन *ausan*, or ओहन *ŏhan*, 'of that kind.'	ओना, *oná* 'in that way.'
Relative		जे *je*, 'who' ...	जैसन *jaisan*, जेहन *jěhan*, 'of what kind.'	जेना *jená*, 'in what way.'
Correlative		से *se*, 'that' ...	तैसन *taisan*, तेहन *těhan*, 'of that kind.'	तेना *tená*, 'in that way.'
Interrogative		के *ke*, 'who?' ...	कैसन *kaisan*, केहन *kěhan*, 'of what kind?'	केना *kená*, 'in what way?'

Pron. adj. of Quantity.	Pron. adv. of Time.	Pron. adv. of Place.	Pron. adv. of Direction.
एत॰ना *ĕt'ná*, 'this much.'	एखनि *ĕkhani*, 'now.'	हियाँ *hiyắ*, 'here.'	इन्दे *indĕ*, इन्ने *inne* or एन्ने *enĕ*, 'hither.'
ओत॰ना *ŏt'ná*, 'that much.'	ओखनि *ŏkhani*, 'then.'	हुआँ *huắ*, 'there.'	उन्दे *undĕ*, उन्ने *unnĕ*, or ओन्ने *onĕ*, 'thither.'
जेत॰ना *jĕt'ná*, 'how much.'	जेखनि *jĕkhani*, 'when.'	जहाँ *jahắ*, 'where.'	जिन्ने *jinnĕ*, 'whither.'
तेत॰ना *tĕt'ná*, 'so much.'	तेखनि *tĕkhani*, 'then.'	तहाँ *tahắ*, 'there.'	तिन्ने *tinnĕ* 'thither.'
केत॰ना *kĕt'ná*, 'how much?'	केखनि *kĕkhani*, 'when?'	कहाँ *kahắ*, 'where?'	किन्ने *kinnĕ*, 'whither?'

§ 33. Adjectival Pronouns.

The following sentences are designed to show the use of the various pronouns, both adjectivally and substantivally. Before doing so it is best to note here that colloquially the oblique forms एह *ĕh*, ओह *ŏh*, जेह *jĕh*, तेह *tĕh*, and केह *kĕh*, are frequently written and pronounced ए *e*, ओ *o*, जे *je*, ते *te*, and के *ke* respectively.

Note that while जे *je* and से *se* are used either as adjectives or substantives in both the nominative and oblique cases, के *ke* cannot be used as an adjective at all. When used as an adjective, के *ke* always becomes कौन *kaun*. Moreover, when used in the *oblique* cases as adjectives, जे *je* or से *se* may optionally become जौन *jaun* or तौन *taun*.

(1) जे ऐलै, से गेलै, *je aïlai, se gĕlai:* 'he who had come, went.'

(2) जे लोग ऐलै, से लोग गेलै, *je log aïlai, se log gĕlai:* 'the man who had come, went.'

(3) जेकर खेत, तेकर धान, *jekar khet, tekar dhán:* 'he who owns the field, owns the paddy.'

(4) जे लोग के खेत, तौन लोग के धान *je log kĕ khet, taun log kĕ dhán:* 'the man who owns the field, owns the paddy.'

(5) के छल *ke chhal?* 'who was it?'

(6) ऊ कौन लोग छिकै *ú kaun log chhikai?* 'what caste is he?'

(7) केकर घोरा छिकै *kekar ghorá chhikai?* 'whose is the horse?'

(8) कौन लोग केर घोरा छिकै *kaun log ker ghorá chhikai?* 'to what people does the horse belong?'

(9) की छिकै *kí chhikai?* 'what is it?'

(10) की गाछ छिकै *kí gáchh chhikai,* 'what tree is it?'

(11) कथी मेँ पानि लैलै है *kathí mẽ páni laïlai hai?* 'in what have you brought the water?'

(12) कौन लोटा मेँ पानि लैलन्हीँ है *kaun loṭá mẽ páni laïl'hí hai?* 'in what *loṭa* have you brought the water?'

(13) केऊ नै ऐलै *kĕú nai aïlai,* 'no one came.'

(14) कोइ लरिका नै ऐलै *koï lariká nai aïlai*, 'no boy came.'

(15) ओहि गाँव मेँ केकऱो किछु नै छै *ŏhi gāw mē kĕk'rŏ kichhu nai chhai*, 'in that village no one has anything.'

(16) ओहि गाँव केर केउ बनियाँ सँ किछु नै मिलऽतै *ŏhi gāw ker kĕú baniyā sē kichhu nai mil'tai*, 'in that village nothing will be got from any shopkeeper.'

(17) ओहि औखद कै केथियो मेँ धरे के* होतै *ŏhi aukhad kai kĕthiyŏ mē dharē ke* hotai*, 'it will be (necessary) to put that medicine into something.'

(18) कै पुरुख ऐला *kai purukh ailá*, 'several men came,' or 'how many men came?'

§ 34. The Pronominal Oblique Genitive.

The following are examples of pronominal genitives which end in र *r* or न *n*, and which have an oblique form ending in रा *rá* or ना *ná*. These oblique forms occur for all pronominal genitives ending in र *r*, and are used with nouns in any form except that of the nominative singular or plural:—

Direct Genitive.	Meaning.	Oblique form.
मोर *mor.*	'My.'	मोरा *morá.*
हमर *hamar.*	'My.'	हमऱा *ham'rá.*
तोर *tor.*	'Thy.'	तोरा *torá.*
तोहर *tohar.*	'Thy.'	तोहऱा *tŏh'rá.*
अप्पन *appan.*	'Own.'	अपऩा *ap'ná.*
एकर *ekar.*	'Of this.'	एकऱा *ĕk'rá.*
ओकर *okar.*	'Of that,' 'his.'	ओकऱा *ŏk'rá.*
जेकर *jekar.*	'Whose.'	जेकऱा *jĕk'rá.*
तेकर *tekar.*	'His.'	तेकऱा *tĕk'rá.*
केकर *kekar.*	'Whose?'	केकऱा *kĕk'rá.*

* Dative of the verbal noun.

The following examples will show the use of the genitive in—(*a*) its direct form, (*b*) its oblique form.

a.—Genitives agreeing with nouns in the nominative form, *i.e.* direct genitives.

ओकर बहु केहन सुन्दर छै *okar bahu kĕhan sundar chhai*, 'how beautiful his wife is!'

केकर बेटा छै *kekar beṭá chhai?* 'whose son is he?'

हमर धन्धा बिगर॰तै *hamar dhandhá bigar'tai*, 'my profession will be ruined.'

ओकर कानब सुन के *okar kánab sun kĕ*, 'on hearing her lamentations.'

ओकर इक॰रार लिखऽ *okar ik'rár likha*, 'write a bond to that effect' (*lit.* of that).

अप्पन धन उड़ाय, भिखारी होय गेल *appan dhan uṛáy, bhikhárí hoy gel*, 'having wasted all his substance, he became poor.'

b.—Genitives agreeing with nouns not in the nominative form, *i.e.* oblique genitives.

ओक॰रा चढ़े के घोरा *ŏk'rá chaṛhĕ kĕ ghorá*, 'his riding-horse' (*lit.* the horse of his riding).

ऊ ओक॰रा फुल॰वारी मेँ ऐलै *ú ŏk'rá phul'wárí mẽ aĭlai*, 'he came into *his* (some one else's) garden.'

हम॰रा सिर॰की मेँ *ham'rá sir'kí mẽ*, 'in my hovel.'

तोह॰रा घर मेँ *tŏh'rá ghar mẽ*, 'in your house.'

तोह॰रा हथ॰वा सेँ *tŏh'rá hath'wá sẽ*, 'from thy hand.'

हम॰रा दर॰वाजा सेँ ओकर दर॰वाजा बाँस भर दूरि छै *ham'rá dar'wájá sẽ okar dar'wájá bā̃s bhar dúri chhai*, 'his doorway is a rod distance from mine.'

किसान अप॰ना जी मेँ बिचार॰लक *kisán ap'ná jí mẽ bichár'lak*, 'the husbandman said in his heart.'

Sometimes, by the vulgar, the direct form is used instead of the oblique, but the oblique form is never used instead of the direct.

DIVISION II.

CONJUGATION.

CHAPTER IV.

INTRODUCTORY.

§ 35. It must be noted with respect to the following paradigms that colloquially the plural is commonly used in the place of the singular: thus तों छह *tõ chha*, 'thou art,' is commonly used instead of तों छैं *tõ chhẽ*, which is the more correct form.

Note also that there is great laxity colloquially in regard to gender. The forms given for the feminine are only those which are specially confined to that gender; but instead of these, the masculine forms are often used colloquially. In the following paradigms when the masculine and feminine forms coincide, the latter are not given. As a matter of fact feminine forms are rarely used except in the west of the district. Perhaps the second plural feminine is the one which is most current.

§ 35*a*. As already observed (§ 1), the language spoken in South Durbhanga, North Munger, and Madhepur is in the main Maithilí. In the eastern portions, however, there is observable a tendency toward the semi-Bangálí of South Bhagalpúr and Purníyá.

§ 36. With regard to the spelling of the various tense-forms, it must be noted that ऐ *ai* and औ *au* are frequently written अइ *aï* and अउ *aü* respectively: thus such forms as देखै *dekhai* and देखौन्ह *dekhaunh* are often written देखइ *dĕkhai̥* and देखउन्ह *dĕkhaünh*. It has not been thought necessary to put both these varieties of spelling into the paradigms: hence only देखै *dekhai*, देखौन्ह *dekhaunh*, &c., will be found therein. With regard to this and to the shortening of ante-penultimate vowels, see General Introduction, §§ 34—37.

It must be noted that a great many verbal forms have a heavy diphthong, viz. ऐ *ai* or औ *au*, in the last syllable. When this occurs in any form (except in the present conjunctive), any preceding long vowel is shortened. Thus we have भेलैक *bhĕlaik*, 'he became,' देखैत *dĕkhait*, 'seeing,' and not भेलैक *bhelaik* or देखैत *dekhait*, as would be required by General Introduction, § 37. In the present conjunctive, however, a preceding vowel remains long, so that we have देखै *dekhai*, '(if) he sees,' and not देखै *dĕkhai*.

Every plural form ending in न्ह *nh* can also be spelt as ending in न *n*: thus गिरलन्ह *gir'lanh* or गिरलन *gir'lan*. Only the fuller form in न्ह *nh* will be given in the paradigms.

When a stem terminates in an unaspirated letter, and is followed by a termination beginning with ह *h*, the final letter of the stem and the initial ह *h* of the termination generally coalesce into the cognate aspirate of the final letter of the stem. Thus देखबन्हो *dĕkhab'ho* becomes देखभो *dĕkh'bho*, and छिकन्हीं *chhik'hī*, छिखीं *chhikhī*.

§ 37. Conjugational System.

The conjugation of the verb √ देख *dekh*, 'see,' being given in full, it is not necessary to give here the details of conjugation at length.

§ 38. There are three moods—the Indicative, Conjunctive, and Imperative. These may again be divided into *simple tenses*—formed from the root direct, and *periphrastic tenses*—formed with the aid of auxiliary verbs added to the present or past participle, or to the conjugated preterite indicative.

§ 39. The *simple tenses* are as follows :—

INDICATIVE.	CONJUNCTIVE.	IMPERATIVE.
Present.	Present.	Present.
Preterite.	Preterite.	
Future.		

Of these, the present imperative is always the same as the present conjunctive.

§ 40. The *periphrastic tenses* are as follows:—

a) From the present participle, direct form—

Indicative—

Definite present	with auxiliary	present.
Imperfect	„	preterite.
Durative future	„	future.

Conjunctive—

Future	with auxiliary	present conjunctive.
Durative present	„	preterite „

b) From the past participle: direct form in the neuter verb, oblique form in the active verb—

Indicative—

Perfect (form II)	with auxiliary	present.
Pluperfect (form II)	„	preterite.
Future exact (form II)	„	future.

Conjunctive—

Future exact (form II)	with auxiliary	present conjunctive.
Preterite (form II)	„	preterite „

c) From the preterite indicative—

Indicative—

Perfect (form I)	with auxiliary	present.
Pluperfect (form I)	„	preterite.
Future exact (form I)	„	future.

Conjunctive—

Future exact (form I)	with auxiliary	present conjunctive.
Preterite (form I)	„	preterite „

Concerning the use of the auxiliary in tenses formed from the past participle, see General Introduction, p. 13, cl. (4).

§ 41. The Simple Tenses.

The personal terminations are nearly the same for all these tenses. They are added to a tense-stem, the formation of which will be described afterwards. They are exactly the same for the present conjunctive, the preterite indicative, and the preterite conjunctive.

The terminations of these three tenses are given in the following table. It will be observed that there are many optional forms of terminations for each person. They are all used with nearly equal frequency. They should be carefully committed to memory.

It must be noted that the termination अह *ah* or अ *a* of the 2nd plural masculine is pronounced with a peculiar drawl, something like the English word 'awe.' Thus, देखअ *dekh*'awe.'

Table showing the Personal Terminations of the Present Conjunctive, the Preterite Indicative, and the Preterite Conjunctive.

Person.	Singular.		Plural.	
	Masculine.	Feminine.	Masculine.	Feminine.
1st	ऊँ *ũ*, ओँ *õ*, औँ *aũ*.		ई *í*, इऐ *iai*, इऐन्ह *iainh*.	ईँ *ĩ*.
2nd	ए *e*, एँ *ẽ*, ऐ *ai*, ऐँ *aĩ*, ऽहीँ *'hĩ*, ऽहीक *'hík*.	ई *í*.	अह *ah*, अ *a*, ऽहौ *'hau*, ऽहौक *'hauk*, ऽहुन्ह *['hunh*.	
3rd	ऐ *ai*, ऐक *aik*, औ *au*, औक *[auk*.		अथ *ath*, अथि *athi*, ऽथिन्ह *'thinh*. ऽहिन्ह *'hinh*. आ *á*. अन्ह *anh*.	ई *í*. इन्ह *inh*.

The first person is often used honorifically in the sense of the second person. Thus आवौँ *áwaũ*, 'come.'

§ 42. These terminations are added to various tense-stems, and it is by these tense-stems that the tenses are distinguished. The formation of each tense-stem will be given separately under the heading of each tense, and the conjugation of each tense will now be described in the order in which they will subsequently be given in the conjugation of the model verb √ देख *dekh*, 'see.'

§ 43. The Preterite Indicative.

The stem of this tense is formed by adding अल *al* to the root. To this the terminations in § 41 are added. Thus √ देख *dekh*, 'see,' preterite stem देखल *dekhal*, to which the terminations are added: thus देखलूँ *děkh'lũ* 'I saw.' This tense has in the case of transitive verbs the following terminations instead of those given in § 41:—अक *ak*, ऽकैक *'kaik*, ऽकौक *'kauk* for the third person singular, and ऽका *'ká*, ऐं *ẽ*, ऽथिन्ह *'thinh*, ऽखिन्ह *'khinh*, अन्ह *anh*, आत *át* in the third person plural masculine, and ऽकी *'kí*, इन्ह *inh*, ईत *it* in the third person plural feminine. In the case of neuter verbs—

(1) the following terminations may be used for the second person singular masculine in addition to those given in § 41:—आ *á*, ऽहैँ *'hãi*, ऽहा *'há*;

(2) in the third singular masculine either no termination is added to the stem at all, or else the following are the terminations:—ए *e*, ऐ *ai*, ऐक *aik*, औ *au*, औक *auk*, and also in North Munger अ *a*;

(3) in the third plural masculine, in addition to the terminations in § 41, the terminations ऐं *ẽ* and आत *át* may be used, and in the feminine, ईत *it*.

In addition to the above, the following terminations may be used in the past tense of all verbs, whether transitive or neuter:—first sing., आँ *ā̃* (only in North Munger); 3rd do., ऽकै *'kai*, ऽकौ *'kau*; first plural, इअन्ह *ianh* and इहन्ह *ihanh*; 2nd do., ऽहठ *'ha*.

Examples.

देखलक *děkh'lak*, देखलऽकैक *děkhal'kaik*, देखलऽकौक *děkhal'kauk*, also देखलऽकै *děkhal'kai*, देखलऽकौ *děkhal'kau*, 'he saw.' देखलऽका *děkhal'ká*, देखलैँ *děkh'lẽ*, देखलऽथिन्ह *děkhal'thinh*, देखलऽखिन्ह *děkhal'khinh*,* देखलन्ह *děkh'lanh*, देखलात *děkh'lát*, 'they saw' (masc.), and देखली *dekh'lí*, देखलिन्ह *děkh'linh*, देखलीत *děkh'lít*, 'they saw' (fem.). Similarly for the other forms.

---

* This is really a contraction of देखलक हिन्ह *dekh'lak hinh*.

§ 44. The Future Indicative.

This tense has two stems—one for the first and second persons, and one for the third person. The first stem is formed by adding अब *ab* to the root; the second is the root itself.

The following are the terminations of this tense. All should be added to the root direct.

After certain vowels, *e.g.* आ *á*, the stem terminations may be एब *ĕb* instead of अब *ab*.

Terminations of the Future.

Person.	Singular.		Plural.	
	Masculine.	Feminine.	Masculine.	Feminine.
1st	॰बौँ *'bõ*, ॰बै *'bai*, ॰बैक *'baik*. ॰बौ *'bau*, ॰बौक *'bauk*.		अब *ab*, ॰बैन्ह *'bainh*.	
2nd	॰बे *'be*, ॰बेँ *'bẽ*, ॰बै *bai*, ॰बैँ *baĩ*. ॰भेँ *'bhẽ*,* ॰भैँ *'bhaĩ*.* ॰भीँ *'bhí*,* ॰भीक *bhík*.*		॰बह *'bah*, ॰बऽ *'ba*. ॰भौ *'bhau*,* ॰भौक *'bhauk*.*	
3rd	अत, ॰तै, ॰तैक, ॰तौ, *at*, *'tai*, *'taik*, *'tau*, ॰तौक *'tauk*.		॰तन्ह *'tanh*. ॰ता *'tá*, ॰तात *'tát*. ॰तथि *'tathi*, ॰थिन्ह *'thinh*.† ॰थनी *'thaní*.†	॰तिन्ह *'tinh*. ॰ती *'tí*, ॰तीत *'tít*.

* These are contractions for ॰ब हेँ *'b hẽ*, ॰ब हैँ *'b haĩ*, &c.

† Contractions for ॰त हिन्ह *'t hinh*, ॰त हनी *'t haní*.

§ 45. The Present Conjunctive and Imperative.

In this tense the terminations are added to the root itself: thus देखूँ *dekhū*, 'let me see.' As already stated, the terminations are those given in § 41. Besides these, this tense may in the third person masculine singular take ए *e* and ओ *o*. It also optionally takes no termination whatever in the second person singular.

In the plural, it may in the first person masculine also take the termination अन्ह *anh*, and in the feminine ऐँ *ãi*, and in the third person the terminations एँ *ẽ*, ऐँ *ãi*, or ऐन्ह *ainh*.

§ 46. The Preterite Conjunctive.

In this tense अत *at* or इत *it* is added to the root to form the stem. The personal terminations in § 41 are then added: thus देख॰तूँ *dĕkh'tū*, '(if) I had seen.'

In the second person singular masculine it also takes the termination आ *á*, and in the third person it may drop the usual terminations and end in ऐत *ait*, added simply to the root: thus देखैत *dĕkhait*. The third person plural masculine also optionally takes the termination हनी *hani*,—thus देख॰थनी *dĕkh'thani* for देखत॰हनी *dĕkhat'hani*. In North Munger and in the Madhepúrá subdivision of Bhagalpúr another form of this tense, founded on a stem देख॰ती *dĕkh'ti* instead of देखत *dekhat*, occurs, which is given in full in the paradigms.

§ 46a. The Use of the Various Verbal Terminations.

It will be noticed that each person has many terminations, but they do not all mean exactly the same thing. At the same time it must be noted that this multiplicity of verbal forms is partly due to local and personal circumstances—an inhabitant of one place using one set of forms, and an inhabitant of another, another. This is due to the want of a literature, which would fix each verbal form in its proper and exact shade of meaning The following instructions will help to explain approximately the more customary uses of the forms.

In the first place it must be noted that in the Maithilí dialect, generally, number is continually disregarded, verbs in the singular form being used with plural subjects, and *vice versâ*. Thus, take देखऽलक *dĕkh'lak*, which is properly third singular preterite. The following examples show that it can be used both in a singular and in a plural sense :—

(Singular) ऊ हमऽरा नदी कात देखऽलक *ú ham'rá nadí kát dĕkh'lak*, 'he saw me beside the river.'

(Plural) ऊ सभ हमऽरा नदी किछार देखऽलक *ú sabh ham'ra nadí kichhár dĕkh'lak*, 'they saw me on the bank of the river.'

So also देखऽलन्ह *dĕkh'lanh* (properly 3rd plural) may be used as a singular : viz. ऊ देखऽलन्ह *ú dĕkh'lanh*, 'he saw,' and ऊ सभ देखऽलन्ह *ú sabh dĕkh'lanh*, 'they saw.' It may be asked, then, why these terminations have been divided into singular and plural. The answer is twofold,—first, that though no longer used in their proper sense, the terminations were originally singular and plural as written, and in songs (which always conserve an older form of the language) they are so used to the present day. Secondly, at the present day there is this important difference in their use,—singular terminations (especially in the second and third persons) are always used non-honorifically, and plural terminations honorifically, as regards the subject; thus, ऊ देखऽलक *ú dĕkh'lak* (singular) means 'he (that humble person) saw,' but ऊ देखऽलन्ह *ú dĕkh'lanh* (plural) means 'he (that respectable person) saw.' In the first person, however, this distinction has been lost, and singular and plural are used indiscriminately.

There is another way of looking at a verbal form, and that is the relation it bears to the object. There is nothing like this in any European language; so it requires more careful exemplification in the present case. For the purposes of the present explanation a sentence may be divided into subject, verb, and object. The object may be direct or remote. Thus, in 'the king gave a village to the bráhman,' 'the king' is the subject, 'gave' is the verb, 'a village' is the direct object, and 'the bráhman' is the remote object. So in 'the child fell on the ground,' for the purposes of the present explanation 'the ground' may be considered as the remote object. In European grammar the form of a verb depends on the subject, *i.e.*, we say that it agrees with its subject in number and person, but the object (direct or remote) has no effect at all on the form of the verb. In Bihárí, on the contrary, the selection of the verbal form to be used largely depends upon the object. Thus, while in Europe we must say that the verb agrees with its subject in number and person, in Bihár we must say that it agrees with its subject, and also with its object, in honour and person.

The following are approximately the rules on this point :—

(*a*) The terminations ending in औ *au* or औक *auk* are used when the object (direct or remote) is in the second person and is considered inferior to the speaker. If, however, the termination is pronounced with a drawl, something like *a-o*, the object is mentioned with some, but not great, respect.

Exception.—If the verb itself is in the second person, the object may be in the first or third person.

(*b*) The terminations ending in ॰ही *'hi*, ऐ *ai*, and ऐक *aik*, are used when the object (direct or remote) is in the first or third person, and is considered inferior to the speaker.

(*c*) The termina tions ending in ऐन्ह *ainh* are used generally when the object (direct or remote) is mentioned with respect.

The following examples will make the above clear :—

First person.—(In this person it must be noted that there is no difference between singular and plural, and that the first person is used instead of the second when respect is intended.)

अहाँ हमर नेना के देख॰लौँ अहि *ahẵ hamar nená ke dĕkh'laũ ahi,* 'has your honour seen my child?' (Here the first person is used honorifically instead of the second person, and no reference being made to the person of or respect due to the object, the form देख॰लिऐ *dĕkh'liai* is not used.)

हम तोहर पोथी बिहान देख॰बौक *ham tohar pothi bihán dĕkh'bauk,* 'I will see your book (my humble friend) to-morrow.' (Here the direct object, 'your book,' being inferior and in the second person, a termination ending in औक *auk* is used.)

एखन्नी जाहौ, आज साँझ के तोहर पाती देखब्बौ *ěkh'ni jáhau, áj sẫjh ke tohar páti děkh'bau* (pronounced *děkh'ba-o*), 'go now, sir; I will see your letter this evening.'

हम अहाँ के देखब्बैन्ह *ham ahẫ ke děkh'bainh*, 'I will see your honour.' (Here the object is mentioned with respect.)

Second Person.—रे छौँड़ा, हमर बही देखले है ? *re chhaũrá, hamar bahi děkh'le hai?* 'Ho! you boy, there, have you seen my book?' (Here the subject is non-honorific, and there is no reference to the object.)

तोँ ओकरा चाकर के देखलन्ही है ? *tõ ŏk'rá chákar ke děkhal'hi hai?* 'Have you (my humble friend) seen his servant?' (Here both subject and object are non-honorific.)

देखलहौक कुकुर नै परा सकलै ? *děkhal'hauk kukur nai pará sak'lai?* 'Did you see the dog (inferior), how it could not run away?'

(Here, although the object is in the third person, still a termination ending in औक *auk* is used, because the subject is in the second person.)

Third person.—देखलहौ मुरता नेना के कैसन चाट खीँच के मारलकै *děkhal'hau Mur'tá nená ke kaisan cháṭ khich kě máral'kai?* 'Did you see how Mur'tá gave a severe slap to the child?' (Here the object, 'the child,' is inferior.)

तोहरा गाड़ी मेँ की माल छौ ? *tŏh'rá gári mẽ ki mál chhau?* (My humble friend), 'what goods are in your cart?'

मजिस्टर साहेब हमरा देखलन्ह *Majisṭar Sáhěb ham'rá děkh'lanh*, 'His Honor, the Magistrate, saw me.'

हो काका, देखलह मोहनक बौह केना डाकलक *ho káká, děkh'lah mŏh'nak bauh kená ḍák'lak?* 'Hallo, uncle, did you see how Mohan's wife called me?'

Regarding the termination हुन्ह *hunh* of the second plural, it is used when the object is in the third person and is spoken of with respect; thus तोँ उन्हकरा देखलहुन्ह *tõ unh'kará děkh'lahunh*, 'you have seen that respected gentleman.'

CHAPTER V.

AUXILIARY VERBS.

§ 47. There are two classes of auxiliary verbs—the *defective* and the *complete.*

§ 48. There are three *defective auxiliary verbs,*—one from the √अहव *ahw* or हव *haw*, another from the √ अछ *achh*, and another from the √ रह *rah*. They are all more or less irregular in their conjugation.

(*a*) The first is used in the third person singular of the present tense only, and loses its initial vowel. I shall call it the *first defective auxiliary verb.*

(*b*) The second is used in the present and preterite tenses, and always loses its initial vowel except in one form, अछ *achh*, of the third singular present. It has in the present tense two forms, a weak (*e.g.* छै *chhai*, 'he is') and a strong (*e.g.* छिकै *chhikai*, 'he is'). In the preterite tense it is used only in the weak form (*e.g.* छलौं *chhalõ*, 'I was'). I shall call it the *second defective auxiliary verb.*

(*c*) The third is used both in the present and preterite tenses,—always, however, with a preterite signification. It is hence classified as a preterite. It has only one form, a weak one (*e.g.* रहो *rahí*, 'I was'). I shall call it the *third defective auxiliary verb.*

§ 49. The complete auxiliary verb is formed from the √ हो *ho* 'become,' which is conjugated through all moods and tenses. Its preterite is irregular, and is never used as an auxiliary, but only as a verb substantive, meaning 'I became.'

§ 50. First Defective Auxiliary Verb.

√ अहु *ahw.*

Present: '*I am,*' *&c.*

Only used in the third person singular masculine, अहि *ahi*, है *hai*, हौ *hau*, or एह *ĕh*, येह *yĕh*, यऽ *ya*, or एहै *ĕhai*, 'he is.' When used as an auxiliary, this is often weakened to हऽ *ha*.

§ 51. Second Defective Auxiliary Verb.

√ अछ *achh*, 'be.'

Present: '*I am,*' *&c.*

WEAK FORM.

Person.	Singular.		Plural.	
	Masculine.	Feminine.	Masculine.	Feminine.
1st	छौँ *chhaũ*,		छी, छिऐ, छिऐन्ह. *chhī*, *chhiai*, *chhiainh*.	छीँ *chhī*.
2nd	छेँ *chhẽ*, छैँ *chhaĩ*, छहीँ *chhahī*.	छी *chhī*.	छह *chhah*, छऽ *chha*, छहौ *chhahau*, छहौक [*chhahauk*.	
3rd	अछ *achh*, छै *chhai*, छैक *chhaik*, छौ *chhau*, छौक *chhauk*.		छथ *chhath*, छथि *chhathi*.	
			छन्ह *chhanh*.	
	छत *chhat*, छैत *chhait*, छौत *chhaut*.		छहिन्ह *chhahinh*, छैन्ह [*chhainh*.	

STRONG FORM.

Person.	SINGULAR.		PLURAL.	
	Masculine.	Feminine.	Masculine.	Feminine.
1st	छिकूँ, छिकोँ, *hhikũ*, *chhikõ*, छिकौँ *chhikaũ*.		छिकी, छिकिऐ, *chhikí*, *chhikiai*, छिकिऐन्ह, *chhikiainh*, छिकन्ह *chhikanh*.	छिकीँ, छिकैँ, *chhikí*, *chhikaĩ*.
2nd	छिके, छिकेँ, छिकै, *chhike*, *chhikẽ*, *chhikai*, छिकैँ *chhikaĩ*. छिखीँ *chhikhí*,* छिखीक [*chhikhík*.*	छिकी *chhikí*.	छिकह, छिकऽ, *chhikah*, *chhika*. छिखौ, छिखौक, *chhikhau*,* *chhikhauk*.* छिखुन्ह *chhikhunh*.*	
3rd	छिकै, छिकैक, *chhikai*, *chhikaik*, छिकौ, छिकौक, *chhikau*, *chhikauk*. छिक, छिके, छिको, *chhik*, *chhike*, *chhiko*.		छिकथ, छिकथि, *chhikath*, *chhikathi*. छिक॰थिन्ह *chhik'thinh*. छिखिन्ह *chhikhinh*.* छिका, छिकेँ, छिकैँ, *chhiká*, *chhikẽ*, *chhikaĩ*. छिकन्ह, छिकैन्ह, *chhikanh*, *chhikainh*.	छिकी *chhikí*. छिकिन्ह, *chhikinh*.

* For छिक॰हीँ ***chhik'hí***, &c., see § 36, last para.

Preterite : '*I was,*' *&c.*

Person.	Singular.		Plural.	
	Masculine.	Feminine.	Masculine.	Feminine.
1st	छलूँ, छलौं, छलौँ, *chhalú̃, chhalõ, chhalaũ.* छलाँ *chhalã́.**		छली, छलिऐ, *chhalí, chhaliai,* छलिऐन्ह *chhaliainh.* छलिअन्ह *chhalianh.* छलिहन्ह *chhalihanh.*	छलीं *chhalí̃.*
2nd	छले, छलेँ, छलै, *chhale, chhalẽ, chhalai,* छलैँ, छलऽहीँ, *chhalaĩ, chhal'hí̃,* छलऽहीक, छला, *chhal'hík, chhalá,* छलऽहैँ, छलऽहा, *chhal'haĩ, chhal'há.*	छली *chhalí.*	छलह *chhalah,* छलऽ *chhala.* छलऽहौ, छलऽहौक, *chhal'hau, chhal'hauk.* छलऽहुन्ह *chhal'hunh.* छलऽहऽ *chhal'ha.*	
3rd	छल *chhal.* छले *chhale.* छलै, छलैक, *chhalai, chhalaik.* छलौ, छलौक, *chhalau, chhalauk.* छलऽकै, छलऽकौ, *chhal'kai, chhal'kau.* छलऽ *chhala.**		छलथ, छलथि, *chhalath, chhalathi,* छलऽथिन्ह *chhal'thinh,* छलऽहिन्ह, *chhal'hinh.* छला *chhalá.* छलन्ह *chhalanh.* छलैँ *chhalẽ.* छलात *chhalát.*	छली *chhalí.* छलिन्ह *chhalinh.* छलीत *chhalít.*

* Peculiar to North Munger.

§ 52. Third Defective Auxiliary Verb.

√ रह *rah*, 'remain.'

Present, *used as a* Preterite: '*I was*,' *&c.*

Person.	Singular.		Plural.	
	Masculine.	Feminine.	Masculine.	Feminine.
1st	रहौँ *rahaũ.*		रही *rahī.*	रहीँ *rahī̃.*
2nd	रहेँ *rahẽ.*	रही *rahī.*	रहऽ *raha.*	
3rd	रहै *rahai.*		रहैन्ह *rahainh.*	रही *rahī.*

Optional forms as in छिकूँ *chhikū̃.*

Preterite: '*I was*,' *&c.*

Person.	Singular.		Plural.	
	Masculine.	Feminine.	Masculine.	Feminine.
1st	रहऽलौँ *rah'laũ.*		रहऽली *rah'lī.*	रहऽलीँ *rah'lī̃.*
2nd	रहऽलेँ *rah'lẽ.*	रहऽली *ra'hlī*	रहऽलऽ *rah'la.*	
3rd	रहल *rahal.*		रहऽलात *rah'lát.*	रहऽलीत *rah'lít.*

Optional forms as in छलूँ *chhalū̃.*

§ 53. The Complete Auxiliary Verb.

√ हो *ho*, '*be*,' '*become*.'

INDICATIVE MOOD.

(*a*)—**Preterite:** '*I became*,' *&c.*

NOTE.—This tense is never used as an auxiliary, छलूँ *chhalū̃* or रही *rahī* (see above) being used instead.

Person.	Singular.		Plural.	
	Masculine.	Feminine.	Masculine.	Feminine.
1st	भेलौं *bhĕlaũ*.		भेली *bhelī*.	भेलीं *bhelī̃*.
2nd	भेलेँ *bhelẽ*.	भेली *bhelī*.	भेलह *bhela*.	
3rd	भेल *bhel*.		भेलात *bhelát*.	भेलीत *bhelīt*.

Optional forms as in छलूँ *chhalū̃*.

The following regular form obtains in the Madhepúrá subdivision of the Bhagalpúr district:—

Person.	Singular.		Plural.	
	Masculine.	Feminine.	Masculine.	Feminine.
1st	होलौं *hc lõ* or होलाँ *holā̃*.		होली *holī*.	होलीं *holī̃*.
2nd	होलेँ *holẽ*.	होली *holī*.	होलह *hola*.	
3rd	होल *hol*.		होलात *holát*.	होलीत *holīt*.

Optional forms as in छलूँ *chhalũ*.

§ 54. (*b*)—Future : '*I shall be,*' *&c.*

Person.	Singular.		Plural.	
	Masculine.	Feminine.	Masculine.	Feminine.
1st	होएबों, होएबै, होएबैक, *hoĕbõ,*hŏĕbai, hŏĕbaik.* होएबौ *hŏĕbau*, होएबौक [*hŏĕbauk.*		होएब *hoĕb*, होएबैन्ह *hŏĕ-* [*bainh.*	
2nd	होएबे, होएबें, *hoĕbe, hoĕbẽ.* होएबै, होएबैं, *hŏĕbai, hŏĕbaĩ.* होएभें *hŏĕbhẽ*, होएभैं [*hŏĕbhaĩ.* होएभी *hŏĕbhí*, होएभीक [*hŏĕbhik.*		होएबह *hoĕbah*, होएबऽ [*hoĕba.* होएभौ *hŏĕbhau*, होएभौक [*hŏĕbhauk.*	
3rd	होअत *hoät.* होतै *hŏtai,*† होतैक [*hŏtaik.*† होतौ *hŏtau,*† होतौक [*hŏtauk.*†		होतन्ह *hotanh,*† होता *hotá,*† होतात *hotát.*† होतथि, होथिन्ह, होथनी, *hotathi,*† *hŏthinh,*† *hŏthaní.*	होतिन्ह *hotinh,*† होती *hotí,*† होतीत [*hotít.*†

* Or होबों *hobõ*, and so throughout.

† Or होअतै *hŏatai*, होय्तै *hŏy'tai*, *&c*

CONJUNCTIVE MOOD.

§ 55. (*c*)—Present: '*(If) I be*,' *&c.*

Person.	Singular.		Plural.	
	Masculine.	Feminine.	Masculine.	Feminine.
1st	होऊँ *hoũ*, होओँ *hoõ*, होअौँ *hoaũ*.		होई *hoī*, होइऐ *hoïai*, होअन्ह *hoanh*.	होई *hoī*, होऐँ *hoaĩ*.
2nd	होए, होएँ, होऐ, होऐँ, *hoe*, *hoẽ*, *hoai*, *hoaĩ*. होहीँ *hohī̃*, होहीक [*hohīk*. हो *ho*.	होइ *hoi*.	होअह *hoah*, होअ *hoa*. होहौ *hohau*, होहौक [*hohauk*. होउन्ह *hohunh*.	
3rd	होऐ *hoai*, होऐक [*hoaik*. होऔ *hóau*, होऔक [*hoauk*. होए *hoë*, होओ *hoö*.		होअथ, होअथि, होथिन्ह, *hoath*, *hoathi*, *hothinh*. होहिन्ह *hohinh*. होआ *hoá*, होअन्ह *hoanh*. होएँ *hoẽ*, होऐँ *hoaĩ*, होऐन्ह [*hoainh*.	होइ *hoi*, होइन्ह *hoïnh*.

§ 56. (*d*)—Preterite: '*(If) I had been,*' *&c.*

Person.	Singular.		Plural.	
	Masculine.	Feminine.	Masculine.	Feminine.
1st	होतूँ *hotũ*, होतौं *hotõ*. होतौँ *hŏtaũ*.		होती *hotí*. होतिऐ *hŏtiaï*.	होतीं *hotĩ*.
2nd	होते, होतें, होतै, होतैं, *hote, hotẽ, hŏtai, hŏtaĩ*, होथीं, होथीक, होता, *hŏthĩ, hŏthik, hotá*.	होती *hoti*.	होतह *hotah*, होतऽ *hota*. होथौ, होथौक, होथुन, *hŏthau, hŏthauk, hŏthun*.	
3rd	होएत *hŏait*. होतै, होतैक, *hŏtai, hŏtaik*, होतौ, होतौक, *hŏtau, hŏtauk*.		होतथ, होतथि, होत॰थिन्ह, *hotath, hotathi, hŏt'thinh*. होथिन्ह, होता, *hŏthinh, hotá*. होतन्ह *hotanh*. होथनी *hothani*.	होती *hoti*. होतिन्ह *hotinh*.

The following forms are used in North Munger and in the Madhepúrá subdivision of Bhagalpúr :—

Person.	Singular.		Plural.	
	Masculine.	Feminine.	Masculine.	Feminine.
1st	होतिहैं *hŏtihaĩ*.	होतीहैं *hŏtihaĩ*.	*No special form.*	
2nd	होतिहै *hŏtihai*. होतिहैं *hŏtihaĩ*.	होतीहै *hŏtihai*. होतीहैं *hŏtihaĩ*.	होतिहौ *hŏtihau*. होतिहौक *hŏtihauk*.	होतीहौ *hŏtihau*. होतीहौक *hŏtihauk*.
3rd	होतिऐ, होतिऐक. *hŏtiai, hŏtiaik*. होतिहत, होतिहैत, *hŏtihat, hŏtihait*, होतिहऽ *hotiha*.		*No special form.*	

§ 57. Imperative Mood.

Present : '*Let me see,*' *&c.*

The same as the present conjunctive.

Precative Forms.

Non-honorific—

होइहौ *hoïhau*, होइभो *hoïbho.*

Honorific—

होइ *hoi*, होइअऽ *hoïya*, 'be good enough to be.'

The periphrastic tenses are quite regular, and need not be given.

§ 58. Present Participle, '*being.*'

Singular and Plural.

होऐत *hŏait.*

Past Participle, '*been.*'

भेल *bhel.*

Conjunctive Participle, '*having been.*'

भै कै *bhai kĕ.*

Infinitive, '*to be.*'

होएब *hoĕb.*

CHAPTER VI.

THE REGULAR ACTIVE VERB.

§ 59. There is only one conjugation of active verbs, if we except a few irregular verbs to be noted further on. The conjugation of neuter verbs differs from that of active verbs only in certain of the past tenses, and these will be treated of in a future page. Verbs whose roots end in vowels also exhibit slight variations, which will be explained at the proper place. For the sake of uniformity the tenses are given in the same order, and under the same names, as those in Dr. Hoernle's Grammar.

Reference is again made to General Introduction, §§ 34 to 36, with regard to the changes of the root-vowel.

§ 60. √देख *dekh*, 'see.'

PRESENT PARTICIPLE: देखैत *dĕkhait*.

PAST PARTICIPLE: देखल *dekhal*.

Simple Tenses.

INDICATIVE MOOD.

§ 61. (*a*)—Preterite: '*I saw,*' *&c.*

Person.	Singular.		Plural.	
	Masculine.	Feminine.	Masculine.	Feminine.
1st	देखऽलूँ *dĕkh'lū̃*, देखऽलोँ [*dĕkh'lõ*. देखऽलौँ *dĕkh'laũ*. देखऽलाँ *dĕkh'lā̃*.*		देखऽली *dĕkh'lī*. देखऽलिऐ *dĕkh'liai*. देखऽलिऐन्ह *dĕkh'liainh*. देखऽलिअन्ह *dĕkh'lianh*. देखऽलिहन्ह *dckh'lihanh*.	देखऽलीँ *dĕkh'lī̃*.
2nd	देखऽले *dĕkh'le*, देखऽलेँ [*dĕkh'lẽ*. देखऽलै, देखऽलैँ, *dĕkh'lai*, *dĕkh'laĩ*, देखलऽहीँ, देखलऽहीक, *dĕkhal'hī̃*, *dĕkhal'hīk*.	देखऽली *dĕkh'lī*.	देखऽलह, देखऽलठ, *dĕkh'lah*, *dĕkh'la*. देखलऽहौ, देखलऽहौक, *dĕkhal'hau*, *dĕkhal'hauk*. देखलऽऊन्ह, देखलऽहठ, *dĕkhal'hunh*, *dĕkhal'ha*.	
3rd	देखऽलक *dĕkh'lak*. देखलऽकै, देखलऽकैक, *dĕkhal'kai*, *dĕkhal'*-[*kaik*. देखलऽकौ, देखलऽकौक, *dĕkhal'kau*, *dĕkhal'*-[*kauk*.		देखलऽका *dĕkhal'kā*, देखऽलैँ [*dĕkh'lẽ*. देखलऽथिन्ह *dĕkhal'thinh*. देखलऽखिन्ह *dĕkhal'khinh*. देखऽलन्ह *dĕkh'lanh*. देखऽलात *dĕkh'lāt*.	देखलऽकी *dĕkhal'kī*. देखऽलिन्ह *dĕkh'linh*. देखऽलीत *dĕkh'līt*.

* Peculiar to North Munger.

§ 62. (*b*)—Future: '*I shall see,*' *&c.*

Person.	Singular.		Plural.	
	Masculine.	Feminine.	Masculine.	Feminine.
1st	देखबों *dĕkh'bõ.* देखबै, देखबैक, *dĕkh'bai, dĕkh'baik.* देखबौ, देखबौक, *dĕkh'bau, dĕkh'bauk.*		देखब, देखबैन्ह, *dekhab, dĕkh'bainh.*	
2nd	देखबे *dĕkh'be,* देखबें [*dĕkh'bẽ.* देखबै *dĕkh'bai,* देखबैं [*dĕkh'bãi.* देखभें *dĕkh'bhẽ,* देखभैं [*dĕkh'bhãi.* देखभीं *dĕkh'bhĩ.* देखभीक *dĕkh'bhik.*		देखबह, देखबऽ, *dĕkh'bah, dĕkh'ba.* देखभौ, देखभौक, *dĕkh'bhau, dĕkh'bhauk.*	
3rd	देखत *dekhat.* देखतै, देखतैक, *dĕkh'tai, dĕkh'taik.* देखतौ, देखतौक, *dĕkh'tau, dĕkh'tauk.*		देखतन्ह *dĕkh'tanh.* देखता *dĕkh'tá.* देखतात *dekh'tát.* देखतथि *dĕkh'tathi.* देखथिन्ह *dĕkh'thinh.* देखथनी *dĕkh'thanī.*	देखतिन्ह *dĕkh'tinh.* देखती *dĕkh'tī.* देखतीत *dĕkh'tīt.*

Honorific forms for second and third persons: देखब *dekhab* or देखबैन्ह *dĕkh'bainh.*

Conjunctive (Conditional) Mood.

§ 63. (*c*)—Present: '*(If) I see;*' rarely '*I see,*' or '*I shall see,*' *&c.*

Person.	Singular. Masculine.	Singular. Feminine.	Plural. Masculine.	Plural. Feminine.
1st	देखूँ *dekhú.*		देखी, दे॑खिऐ, दे॑खिऐन्ह, *dekhí, dĕkhiai, dĕkhiainh.*	देखी *dekhí.*
1st	देखौं, देखौँ, *dekhõ, dekhãũ.*		देखन्ह *dekhanh.*	देखैँ *dekhãĩ.*
2nd	देख, देखे, देखेँ, *dekh, dekhe, dekhẽ,*	देखी *dekhí.*	देखह, देखऽ, *dekhah, dekha.*	
2nd	देखै *dekhai,* देखैँ *dekhãĩ.*		दे॑खऽहौ, दे॑खऽहौक, *dĕkh'hau, dĕkh'hauk.*	
2nd	दे॑खऽहीँ, दे॑खऽहीक, *dekh'hí, dĕkh'hík.*		दे॑खऽहुन्ह *dĕkh'hunh.*	
3rd	देखै, देखैक, *dekhai, dekhaik.*		देखथ, देखथि, *dekhath, dekhathi.*	
3rd	देखौ, देखौक, *dekhau, dekhauk.*		दे॑खऽथिन्ह, दे॑खऽहिन्ह, *dĕkh'thinh, dĕkh'hinh.*	
3rd			देखा, देखन्ह, *dekhá, dekhanh.*	देखी *dekhí,* देखिन्ह *dekhinh.*
3rd	देखे *dekhe,* देखो *dekho.*		देखेँ, देखैँ, देखैन्ह, *dekhẽ, dekhãĩ, dekhainh.*	

§ 64. (*d*)—Preterite: '(*If*) *I had seen,*' *&c.*

Person.	Singular.		Plural.	
	Masculine.	Feminine.	Masculine.	Feminine.
1st	देख॰तूँ, देख॰तों, *dĕkh'tū̃,** *dĕkh'tõ.* देख॰तौँ *dĕkh'taũ.*		देख॰ती *dĕkh'tī.* देख॰तिऐ *dĕkh'tiai,* देख॰तिऐन्ह *dĕkh'tiainh.*	देख॰तीं *dĕkh'tī̃.*
2nd	देख॰ते, देख॰तेँ, *dĕkh'te, dekh'tẽ.* देख॰तै, देख॰तैँ, *dĕkh'tai, dekh'taĩ.* देख॰थीं, देख॰थीक, *dĕkh'thī̃, dĕkh'thīk,* देख॰ता *dĕkh'tá.*	देख॰ती *dĕkh'tī.*	देख॰तह *dĕkh'tah.* देख॰त० *dĕkh'ta.* देख॰थौ, देख॰थौक, *dĕkh'thau, dĕkh'thauk,* देख॰थुन्ह *dĕkh'thunh.*	
3rd	देखैत *dĕkhait.* देख॰तै, देख॰तैक, *dĕkh'tai, dĕkh'taik,* देख॰तौ, देख॰तौक, *dĕkh'tau, dĕkh'tauk.*		देख॰तथ, देख॰तथि, *dĕkh'tath, dĕkh'tathi,* देखत॰थिन्ह *dĕkhat'thinh.* देख॰थिन्ह, देख॰ता, *dĕkh'thinh, dĕkh'tá:* देख॰तन्ह, देख॰थनी. *dĕkh'tanh, dĕkh'thanī.*	देख॰ती *dĕkh'tī.* देख॰तिन्ह *dĕkh'tinh.*

* Or देखितूँ *dĕkhitū̃*, and so throughout.

The following forms are used in North Munger and in the Madhepúrá subdivision of Bhagalpúr :—

Person.	Singular.		Plural.	
	Masculine.	Feminine.	Masculine.	Feminine.
1st	देख॰तिऐँ *dĕkh'tihaĩ.*	देख॰तीऐँ *dĕkh'tīhaĩ.*	*No special form.*	
2nd	देख॰तिऐ *dĕkh'tihai.*	देख॰तीऐ *dĕkh'tīhai.*	देख॰तिऔ *dĕkh'tihau.*	देख॰तीऔ *dĕkh'tīhau.*
	देख॰तिऐँ *dĕkh'tihaĩ.*	देख॰तीऐँ *dĕkh'tīhaĩ.*	देख॰तिहौक *dĕkh'tihauk.*	देख॰तीऔक *dĕkh'tī-hauk.*
3rd	देख॰तिऐ, देख॰तिऐक, *dĕkh'tiai, dĕkh'tiaik.*		*No special form.*	
	देख॰तिअत, देख॰तिहैत, *dĕkh'tihat, dĕkh'tihait.*			
	देख॰तिअ॰ *dĕkh'tiha.*			

IMPERATIVE MOOD.

§ 65. (*e*)—Present.—Same as Present Conjunctive.

Precative Forms.

Non-honorific—

2nd person : देखिऔ *dĕkhihau*, देखिभो *dĕkhibho.*

Honorific—

2nd person : देखी *dekhi*, देखिअ॰ *dĕkhiya.*

(B)–Periphrastic Tenses.

INDICATIVE MOOD.

§ 66. In the following paradigms the optional forms and dialectic forms of the auxiliary verbs will not all be given, as taking up too much valuable space. For similar reasons feminine forms are generally omitted. When not given, they only differ from the masculine in assuming the feminine form of the auxiliary verb. Thus the first plural definite present is—masculine देखैछी *dĕkhaichhī* and feminine देखैछीं *dĕkhaichhī*.

§ 67. (*g*)—Definite Present: '*I am seeing,*' *&c.*

Person.	Singular.	Plural.
1st	देखैछौं *dĕkhaichhaũ.*	देखैछी *dĕkhaichhī.*
2nd	देखैछें *dĕkhaichhĕ̃.*	देखैछऽ *dĕkhaichha.*
3rd	देखैछै *dĕkhaichhai* or देखैयऽ *dĕkhaiya.*	देखैछैन्ह *dĕkhaichhainh.*

§ 68. To form the feminine, use feminine forms of the auxiliary verb. Thus, second singular देखैछी *dĕkhaichhī*, first plural देखैछीं *dĕkhaichhī*.

Any optional form of the present of the defective auxiliary verb may be used; also the strong form of the defective auxiliary verb. Thus, first plural, देखैछिऐ *dĕkhaichhiai* or देखैछिकी *dĕkhaichhikī*. Before these auxiliary verbs the final त *t* of the present participle may optionally be retained. The participle and auxiliary are then written as two words: thus, first plural देखैत छी *dĕkhait chhī*, देखैत छिकी *dĕkhait chhikī*.

§ 69. (*i*)—Imperfect : '*I was seeing.*'

Person.	Singular.	Plural.
1st	देखैछलौं *děkhaichhalõ.*	देखैछली *děkhaichhalí.*
2nd	देखैछलैं *děkhaichhalẽ.*	देखैछल *děkhaichhala.*
3rd	देखैछल *děkhaichhal.*	देखैछला *děkhaichhalá.*

To form the feminine, use feminine forms of the auxiliary verb, as in the definite present.

Any optional form of the preterite of the defective auxiliary verb may be used. Also the third defective auxiliary verb in the present (preterite) tense: thus, first plural देखैरही *děkhairahí.* Before these auxiliaries the final त *t* of the present participle may optionally be retained. The participle and auxiliary are then written as two words: thus, first plural देखैत छली *děkhait chhalí.*

§ 70. (*j*)—Durative Future : '*I shall be seeing,*' &c.

Person.	Singular.	Plural.
1st	देखैहोएबैक *děkhaihŏěbaik.*	देखैहोएब *děkhaihoěb.*
2nd	देखैहोएबैं *děkhaihoěbẽ.*	देखैहोएब *děkhaihoěba.*
3rd	देखैहोअत *děkhaihoät.*	देखैहोता *děkhaihotá.*

To form the feminine, use feminine forms of the auxiliary verb, as in the definite present.

Any optional form of the future of the complete auxiliary verb may be used throughout. Before the auxiliary the final त *t* of the present participle may optionally be retained. The participle and auxiliary are then written as tow words: thus, first plural देखैत होएब *dekhait hoěb.*

§ 71. (*k*)—Perfect: '*I have seen,*' &c.

This tense has two forms of conjugation, used with equal frequency.

FORM I.

Person.	Singular.	Plural.
1st	देखऽलौं यऽ *dĕkh'lõ ya.*	देखऽली यऽ *dĕkh'lí ya.*
2nd	देखऽलैं यऽ *dĕkh'lẽ ya.*	देखऽलऽ यऽ *dĕkh'la ya.*
3rd	देखऽलक यऽ *dĕkh'lak ya.*	देखलऽका यऽ *dĕkhal'ká ya.*

To form the feminine, use feminine forms of the preterite: thus, second singular feminine देखऽली यऽ *dĕkh'li ya.*

Any optional form of the preterite may be used. हऽ *ha* or है *hai* may be substituted for यऽ *ya* throughout.

The word यऽ *ya* in this tense has a peculiar pronunciation, something like the English word 'yaw.'

FORM II.

Person.	Singular.	Plural.
1st	देखऽले * छौं *dekh'le chhaũ.*	देखऽले छी *dĕkh'le chhi.*
2nd	देखऽले छैं *dĕkh'le chhẽ.*	देखऽले छऽ *dĕkh'le chha.*
3rd	देखऽले छै *dĕkh'le chhai.*	देखऽले छैन्ह *dĕkh'le chhainh.*

* Or देखऽलऽ *dĕkh'la*, and so throughout.

To form the feminine, use feminine forms of the auxiliary verb: thus, second singular feminine देखऽले छी *dĕkh'le chhi*, and so on, as in the definite present.

As in the definite present, any optional form of the present of the defective auxiliary verb may be used, and also the strong form of the defective auxiliary verb: thus, first plural देख॰लें छिऐ *dĕkh'le chhiai*, देख॰ले छिकी *dĕkh'le chhiki*, and so on.

§ 72. (*l*)—Pluperfect: '*I had seen*,' &c.

This also, like the perfect, has two forms of conjugation.

FORM I.

Person.	Singular.	Plural.
1st	देख॰लौँ रहे *dĕkh'lõ rahe.*	देख॰ली रहे *dĕkh'lĭ rahe.*
2nd	देख॰लैँ रहे *dĕkh'lẽ rahe.*	देख॰लह रहे *dĕkh'la rahe.*
3rd	देख॰लक रहे *dĕkh'lak rahe.*	देखल॰का रहे *dĕkhal'ká rahe.*

To form the feminine, use feminine forms of the preterite: thus, second singular feminine देख॰ली रहे *dĕkh'lĭ rahe.*

Any of the other forms of the preterite may be used throughout.

FORM II.

Person.	Singular.	Plural.
1st	देख॰ले* छलौँ *dĕkh'le chhalõ.*	देख॰ले छली *dĕkh'le chhalĭ.*
2nd	देख॰ले छलैँ *dĕkh'le chhalẽ.*	देख॰ले छलह *dĕkh'le chhala.*
3rd	देख॰ले छल *dĕkh'le chhal.*	देख॰ले छला *dĕkh'le chhalá.*

* Or देख॰लह *dĕkh'la*, and so throughout.

To form the feminine, use feminine forms of the auxiliary, as in the imperfect.

Any optional form of the preterite of the second defective auxiliary verb may be used; also the third defective auxiliary verb in the present (preterite) tense: thus, first plural देख॰ले रही *dĕkh'le rahí*, and so on.

§ **73.** (*m*)—**Future Exact** : '*I shall have seen,*' '*I may have seen,*' *&c.*

This tense also has two forms of conjugation.

FORM I.

Person.	Singular.	Plural.
1st	देखल्हौं होयत *dĕkh'lŏ hoät.*	देखल्ही होयत *dĕkh'li hoät.*
2nd	देखल्हें होयत *dĕkh'lẽ hoät.*	देखल्हऽ होयत *dĕkh'la hoät.*
3rd	देखलक होयत *dĕkh'lak hoät.*	देखलका होयत *dĕkhal'ká hoät.*

To form the feminine, use feminine forms of the preterite : thus, second singular feminine, देखल्ही होयत *dĕkh'li'hoät.*

FORM II.

Person.	Singular.	Plural.
1st	देखले * होएबैक *dĕkh'le hŏĕbaik.*	देखले होएब *dĕkh'le hoĕb.*
2nd	देखले होएबैं *dĕkh'le hoĕbẽ.*	देखले होएबऽ *dĕkh'le hoĕba.*
3rd	देखले होयत *dĕkh'le hoät.*	देखले होता *dĕkh'le hotá.*

* Or देखलऽ *dĕkh'la*, and so throughout.

To form the feminine, use feminine forms of the auxiliary verb, as in the definite present.

Any other form of the future of the complete auxiliary verb may be used instead throughout.

CONJUNCTIVE (CONDITIONAL) MOOD.

§ 74. (n)—Future Conditional : '(If) I be seeing,' &c.

Person.	Singular.	Plural.
1st	देखैहोऊँ *dĕkhaihoū̃.*	देखैहोई *dĕkhaihoī.*
2nd	देखैहोएँ *dĕkhaihoẽ.*	देखैहोअ *dĕkhaihoa.*
3rd	देखैहोऐ *dĕkkaihoai.*	देखैहोऐन्ह *dĕkhaihoainh.*

To form the feminine, use feminine forms of the auxiliary verb.

Any other form of the present of the complete auxiliary verb may be used instead throughout. Before the auxiliary, the final त *t* of the present participle may optionally be retained. The participle and auxiliary are then written as two words: thus, first plural, देखैत होई *dĕkhait hoī.*

§ 75. (o)—Durative Present Conditional: '(If) I were seeing,' &c.

Person.	Singular.	Plural.
1st	देखैहोतौं *dĕkhaihotŏ̃.*	देखैहोती *dĕkhaïhotī.*
2nd	देखैहोतेँ *dĕkhaihotẽ.*	देखैहोतह *dĕkhaïhota.*
3rd	देखैहोऐत *dĕkhaihŏait.*	देखैहोता *dĕkhaihotá.*

To form the feminine, use feminine forms of the auxiliary verb.

Any other form of the preterite conditional of the complete auxiliary verb may be used instead throughout. Before the auxiliary, the final त *t* of the present participle may optionally be retained. The participle and auxiliary are then written as two words: thus, first plural, देखैत होती *dekhait hoti.*

§ 76. (*p*)—Future Exact Conditional: '(*If*) *I have seen,*' &c.

This tense also has two forms of conjugation.

FORM I.

Person.	Singular.	Plural.
1st	देखल्लौं होऐ *dĕkh'lŏ hoai.*	देखल्ली होऐ *dĕkh'li hoai.*
2nd	देखल्लैँ होऐ *dĕkh'le hoai.*	देखल्ल होऐ *dĕkh'la hoai.*
3rd	देखल्लक होऐ *dĕkh'lak hoai.*	देखलल्का होऐ *dĕkhal'ká hoai.*

To form the feminine, use feminine forms of the preterite: thus, second singular feminine, देखल्ली होऐ *dĕkh'li hoai.*

FORM II.

Person.	Singular.	Plural.
1st	देखल्ले* होऊँ *dĕkh'le hoû.*	देखल्ले होइ *dĕkh'le hoi.*
2nd	देखल्ले होएँ *dĕkh'le hoĕ.*	देखल्ले होअ *dĕkh'le hoa.*
3rd	देखल्ले होऐ *dĕkh'le hoai.*	देखल्ले होऐन्ह *dĕkh'le hoainh.*

* Or देखल्लऽ *dĕkh'la,* and so throughout.

To form the feminine, use feminine forms of the auxiliary verb.

Any other form of the present of the complete auxiliary verb may be used instead throughout.

§ 77. (*q*)—Preterite Conditional: '(*If*) *I had seen*,' *&c.*

This tense also has two forms of conjugation.

FORM I.

Person.	Singular.	Plural.
1st	देखल्लों होएत *děkh'lõ hŏait.*	देखल्ली होएत *děkh'li hŏait.*
2nd	देखल्लँ होएत *děkh'lẽ hŏait.*	देखल्लऽ होएत *děkh'la hŏait.*
3rd	देखल्लक होएत *děkh'lak hŏait.*	देखलन्का होएत *děkhal'ká hŏait.*

To form the feminine use feminine forms of the preterite: thus, second singular feminine देखल्ली होएत *děkh'li hŏait.*

FORM II.

Person.	Singular.	Plural.
1st	देखल्ले* होतौं *děkh'le hotõ.*	देखल्ले होती *děkh'le hoti.*
2nd	देखल्ले होतेँ *děkh'le hotẽ.*	देखल्ले होतऽ *děkh'le hota.*
3rd	देखल्ले होएत *děkh'le hŏait.*	देखल्ले होता *děkh'le hotá.*

* Or देखल्लऽ *děkh'la*, and so throughout.

To form the feminine, use feminine forms of the auxiliary verb.

Any other form of the preterite conditional of the complete auxiliary verb may be used instead throughout.

§ 78. Participles.

ADJECTIVAL.

Present, 'seeing' . . . { देखत *dekhat; obl.* देख॰ते *dĕkh'te* or देख॰तऽ *dĕkh'ta.*
देखैत *dĕkhait.*

Past, 'seen' . . . . . { *a*) देखल *dekhal;* fem. देख॰ली *dĕkh'li; obl.* देख॰ले *dĕkh'le* or देख॰लऽ *dĕkh'la.*
b) देखल भेल *dekhal bhel.*

CONJUNCTIVE.

'Having seen' . . . . देख* के *dekh kĕ,* -कै *-kai,* -कँ *-kẽ,* or -कैँ *-kaĩ.*

§ 79. Infinitives or Verbal Nouns, *'to see,' 'the act of seeing.'*

Nominative.	Oblique.
देख *dekh,** देखि *dekhi.*	देखे *dekhĕ,* देखै *dekhaĭ,* or देखऽ *dekha.*
देखल *dekhal.*	देख॰ला *dĕkh'lá.*
देखब *dekhab.*	देख॰बा *dĕkh'bá.*

§ 80. Noun of Agency, *'one who sees.'*

देख॰निहार *dĕkh'nihár,* देखन॰वाला *dĕkhan'wálá,* or देख॰वैया *dĕkh'waiyá.*

---

* This form of the verbal noun is always the same as the root. So also in the conjunctive participle.

CHAPTER VII.

THE REGULAR NEUTER VERB.

§ 81. This verb differs from the active verb only in the formation of certain of its past tenses. The three more usual past tenses are here given; the conjugation of the rest of the verb can be learnt from the conjugation of the √ देख *dekh*.

NOTE that throughout the periphrastic tenses of the neuter verb, in which the past participle occurs, the past participle takes the direct form गिरल *giral*, fem. गिरल्ली *gir'li*, not an oblique form गिरल्ले *gir'le* or गिरल्लउ *gir'la*, which might be expected: thus हम गिरल होएब *ham giral hoĕb* (fem. हम गिरल्ली होएब *ham gir'li hoĕb*), 'I shall have fallen,' and not हम गिरल्ले होएब *ham gir'le hoĕb*, 'I shall have fallen.'

§ 82. √ गिर *gir*, 'fall.'

PAST PARTICIPLE: गिरल *giral*, fem. गिरल्ली *gir'li*; obl. गिरल *giral*.

Indicative Mood.

§ 83. (*a*) Preterite: '*I fell,*' *&c.*

Person.	Singular.		Plural.	
	Masculine.	Feminine.	Masculine.	Feminine.
1st	गिरऽलूँ, गिरऽलों, *gir'lú, gir'lõ,* गिरऽलौँ, *gir'lãu.* गिरऽलाँ, *gir'lã́.**		गिरऽली *gir'li.* गिरऽलिऐ *gir'liai,* गिरऽलिऐन्ह *gir'liainh.* गिरऽलिअन्ह, गिरऽलिहन्ह, *gir'lianh, gir'lihanh.*	गिरऽलीँ *gir'lĩ.*
2nd	गिरऽले, गिरऽलेँ, *gir'le, gir'lẽ,* गिरऽलै, गिरऽलैँ, *gir'lai, gir'lãi.* गिरलऽहीँ, गिरलऽहीक. *giral'hí, giral'hík.* गिरऽला, गिरलऽहैँ, *gir'lá, giralhãi,* गिरलऽहा *giral'há.*	गिरऽली *gir'li.*	गिरऽलह *gir'lah.* गिरऽलऽ *gir'la.* गिरलऽहौ, गिरलऽहौक. *giral'hau, giral'hauk.* गिरलऽहुन्ह *giral'hunh.* गिरलऽहऽ *giral'ha.*	
3rd	गिरल *giral*, गिरऽले [*gir'le.* गिरऽलै, गिरऽलैक, *gir'lai, gir'laik.* गिरऽलौ, गिरऽलौक, *gir'lau, gir'lauk.* गिरलऽकै, गिरलऽकौ, *giral'kai, giral'kau.* गिरलऽ *girala.**		गिरऽलथ *gir'lath,* गिरऽलथि, *gir'lathi,* गिरऽलऽथिन्ह, *gir'l'thinh,* गिरलऽहिन्ह, *giral'hinh,* गिरऽला *gir'lá.* गिरऽलन्ह *gir'lanh.* गिरऽलेँ *gir'lẽ.* गिरऽलात *gir'lát.*	गिरऽली *gir'li.* गिरऽलिन्ह *gir'linh.* गिरऽलीत *gir'lit.*

* Peculiar to North Munger.

§ 84. (*k*)—Perfect : '*I have fallen,*' *&c.*

FORM I.

Person.	Singular.	Plural.
1st	गिरल्हौँ यठ *gir'lŏ ya.*	गिरल्ही यठ *gir'li ya.*
2nd	गिरल्हेँ यठ *gir'lĕ ya.*	गिरल्हठ यठ *gir'la ya.*
3rd	गिरल यठ *giral ya.*	गिरल्हा यठ *gir'lá ya.*

To form the feminine, use feminine forms of the preterite : thus, second singular feminine गिरल्ही यठ *gir'lí ya.*

Any of the other forms of the preterite may be used throughout. यठ *ha* or है *hai* may be substituted for यठ *ya* throughout.

The word यठ *ya* in this tense has a peculiar pronunciation, something like that of the English word 'yaw.'

FORM II.

This form means, '*I am fallen,*' rather than '*I have fallen.*'

Person.	Singular.	Plural.
1st	गिरल छौँ *giral chhaũ.*	गिरल छी *giral chhí.*
2nd	गिरल छेँ *giral chhĕ.*	गिरल छठ *giral chha.*
3rd	गिरल छै *giral chhai.*	गिरल छैन्ह *giral chhainh.*

To form the feminine, use feminine forms of the past participle and of auxiliary : thus, second singular feminine गिरल्ही छी *gir'lí chhí*, and so on.

Any optional form of the present of the defective auxiliary verb may be used, and the strong form of the defective auxiliary verb: thus, गिरल छिऐ *giral chhiai*, गिरल छिकी *giral chhiki*, *&c.*

§ 85. (*l*)—Pluperfect: '*I had fallen,*' *&c.*

FORM I.

Person.	Singular.	Plural.
1st	गिर॰लौं रहे *gir'lõ rahe.*	गिर॰ली रहे *gir'li rahe.*
2nd	गिर॰लैं रहे *gir'lẽ rahe.*	गिर॰लह रहे *gir'la rahe.*
3rd	गिरल रहे *giral rahe.*	गिर॰ला रहे *gir'lá rahe.*

To form the feminine, use feminine forms of the preterite: thus, second singular feminine गिर॰ली रहे *gir'li rahe.*

Any of the other forms of the preterite may be used throughout.

FORM II.

This form means '*I was fallen,*' rather than '*I had fallen.*'

Person.	Singular.	Plural.
1st	गिरल छलौं *giral chhalõ*	गिरल छली *giral chhalí.*
2nd	गिरल छलैं *giral chhalẽ.*	गिरल छलह *giral chhala.*
3rd	गिरल छल *giral chhal.*	गिरल छला *giral chhalá.*

To form the feminine, use feminine forms of the past participle and auxiliary: thus, second singular feminine गिर॰ली छली *gir'li chhali*, and so on.

Any optional form of the preterite of the second auxiliary verb may be used; also the third auxiliary verb in the present (preterite) tense: thus, first plural गिरल रही *giral rahí*, and so on.

CHAPTER VIII.

VOCALIC ROOTS.

§ 86. Many verbs have roots ending in vowels, and the junction of the root with the termination frequently causes some slight apparent irregularity.

For this reason the following examples are given of the conjugation of verbs having roots ending in vowels. They are here conjugated in the masculine gender, and through the four radical and participial tenses. * From these the periphrastic tenses can easily be formed. It has not been thought necessary to give the conjugation in full for each person.

With regard to the shortening of the root-vowel, see General Introduction, § 36.

§ 87. Example of a verb whose root ends in आ *á* :—

The conjugation of these verbs should be carefully studied, as a large class of active and causal verbs follows it.

In the preterite indicative these verbs insert a junction vowel between the root and the ल *l* of the termination: thus ख* + ए + लोँ *kha* + *ĕ* + *lõ*, or खैलोँ *khailõ*, 'I ate,' where ए *ĕ* is the junction vowel; and प* + ओ + लोँ *pa* + *ŏ* + *lõ*, or पौलोँ *paulõ*, 'I got,' where ओ *ŏ* is the junction vowel. As will be subsequently seen, the same peculiarity exists in other tenses besides the preterite.

The following rules show when ए *ĕ* and when ओ *ŏ* is the junction vowel:—

1) All active (including causal) verbs take ओ *ŏ* : thus पौलोँ* *paulõ* 'I got;' चढ़ौलोँ *charhaulõ*, 'I caused to ascend.'

Exception.—The root √ खा *khá*,* 'eat,' always takes ए *ĕ* : thus खैलोँ *khailõ* , 'I ate.'

---

* With regard to the shortening of the root-vowel and contraction of concurrent vowels, see General Introduction, §§ 34, 36.

2) All neuter verbs take ए *ĕ*: thus अघैलौं *aghailŏ*, 'I was satiated.'

Exception.—The √ गा *gá*, 'sing,' always takes ओ *o*: thus गौलौं *gaulŏ*, 'I sang.'

It is usual to add the letter व *w* to the end of all roots which take ओ *ŏ* in order to distinguish them from those which take the letter ए *ĕ*: thus √ पाव *páw*, √ गाव *gáw*, *&c.*, which take ओ *ŏ*; but √ अघा *aghá*, आ *á*, *&c.*, which take ए *ĕ*.

NOTE.—The √ आ *á*, 'come,' is irregular, in that it takes ओ *ŏ* as its junction vowel in the present participle and the preterite conjunctive, while it takes ए *ĕ* as its junction vowel in the preterite indicative and connected forms.

All verbs which take ओ *ŏ* in the preterite indicative insert व *w* in the past participle; and similarly all verbs which take ए *ĕ*, insert it also in the past participle and in that form of the 3rd singular preterite which is the same as the past participle.

All these verbs generally take ए *ĕ* as the junction vowel in the future indicative. Sometimes, however, verbs which in other tenses take ओ *ŏ* as the junction vowel do so also in this tense: thus, ई भलाइ केर बद॰ला तोह॰रा कै एक बात बतौबौ (instead of बतैबौ) *ī bhaláï ker bad'lá tŏh'rá kai ĕk bát bataubau* (instead of *bataibau*).

§ 88. The following examples will make the above remarks clear.

The easiest way of remembering these changes is to note the form of the past participle of each verb, and then, as explained in General Introduction, § 37, the व *wa* or ए *ĕ* is weakened in certain cases to ओ *ŏ* or इ *i* respectively.

It must, however, be noted that even in active verbs there is a tendency to substitute य *ya* for व *wa*, so that we sometimes find forms like पैलों *pailõ* instead of पौलों *paulõ*. This tendency, moreover, becomes the rule to the east of North Munger and in the Madhepúrá subdivision of Bhagalpúr, where the people always say पैलों *pailõ*, बजैलों *bajailõ*, गैलों *gailõ*, &c., and never पौलों *paulõ*, बजौलों *bajaulõ*, गौलों *gaulõ*, &c.

Many people write इ *i* instead of ए *ĕ* and उ *u* instead of ओ *ŏ*: thus अइलों *aïlõ* instead of अएलों *aĕlõ* for ऐलों *ailõ*, and पउलों *paülõ* instead of पओलों *paŏlõ* for पौलों *paulõ*. Cf. § 39 of this part, and § 35 of the General Introduction. The word for 'he came' is always आएल *áĕl*, and never आइल *áïl*. See § 96.

Many people also write ओ *ŏ* instead of व *wa* in the past participle. Thus, it is quite common to find the words in the second column of the opposite table spelt पाओल *páŏl*, बजाओल *bajáŏl*, चढ़ाओल *charháŏl*, गाओल *gáŏl*.

§ 89. √पा *pá*, 'get.'

INFINITIVE (1ST FORM): पा *pá*; obl. पाए *páĕ*, पावे *páwĕ*, पावऽ *páwa*, or पा *pá*.

" (2ND FORM): पावल *páwal*; obl. पौला *paulá*.* (See General Introduction, § 37.)

" (3RD FORM): पाएब *páĕb*; obl. पैबा *paibá*, 'to get.'

PRES. PART. पवैत *pawait*.†

---

* But from √खा *khá*, खाएल *kháĕl*, obl. खैला *khailá*, and so also in other verbs whose junction vowel is ए *ĕ*, and in the case of all verbs to the east of North Munger and in Madhepúrá.

† But from √खा *khá*, खाइत *kháït* or खात *khát*, and so also in other verbs whose junction vowel is ए *ĕ*, except √आ *á*, 'come,' which makes आवत *áwat* or अवैत *await*. To the east of North Munger and in Madhepúrá, all verbs follow √खा *khá*.

INDICATIVE MOOD.

Person.	Preterite. (See remarks above.)		Future.	
	Singular.	Plural.	Singular.	Plural.
1st	पौलों *paulõ.*	पौली *paulí.*	पैबों *paibõ.*	पाएब *páĕb.*
2nd	पौलें *paulẽ.*	पौलऽ *paula.*	पैबें *paibẽ.*	पैबऽ *paiba.*
3rd	पौलक *paulak.*	पौलन्का *paŭl'ká.*	पौतै *pautai.**	पौता *pautá.*

* But खैतै *khaitai* or खातै *khátai*, and so also in other verbs whose junction vowel is ए *ĕ*, and in the case of all verbs to the east of North Munger and in Madhepúrá.

CONDITIONAL MOOD.

Person.	Present.		Preterite.	
	Singular.	Plural.	Singular.	Plural.
1st	पाऊँ *páũ.*	पाइ *pái.*	पौतों *pautõ.**	पौती *pautí.*
2nd	पावें *páwẽ.*	पावऽ *páwa.*	पौतें *pautẽ.*	पौतऽ *pauta.*
3rd	पावै *páwai.*	पावैन्ह *páwainh.*	पवैत *pawait.*	पौता *pautá.*

* But from √ खा *khá*, खैतों *khaitõ* or खातों *khátõ*, and so on throughout (the third singular being खाइत *kháït* or खात *khát*) for all verbs whose junction vowel is ए *ĕ*, except the √ आ *á*, 'come.' To the east of North Munger, and in Madhepúrá, all verbs follow √ खा *khá*.

To recapitulate,—

It will be seen that verbs whose junction vowel is ए *ĕ* omit व *w* in the present participle and the preterite conditional. In these forms also they optionally insert इ *i*. The only exception is the √ आ *á*, 'come,' which retains the व *w* in these cases, though it takes ए *ĕ*, and not ओ *ŏ*, in the past participle and tenses formed therefrom. In short, the √ आ *á* is conjugated like a verb whose junction vowel is ओ *ŏ* in the present participle and its derived forms, but like a verb whose junction vowel is ए *ĕ* in the past participal and its derived forms.

§ 90. Example of a verb whose root ends in ई *í*:—

√पी *pí*, 'drink.'

INFINITIVE (2ND FORM): पीअल *píal* or पील *píl*, 'to drink.'
PRES. PART. पिबैत *pibait* or पीत *pít*.

INDICATIVE MOOD.

Person.	Preterite.		Future.	
	Singular.	Plural.	Singular.	Plural.
1st	पीलौं *pílõ*.*	पीली *píli*.	पीबौं *píbõ*.†	पीअब *píab*.
2nd	पीलेँ *pílẽ*.	पीलऽ *píla*.	पीबेँ *píbẽ*.	पीबऽ *píba*.
3rd	पिलन्कै *pil'kai*.	पिलन्का *pil'ká*.	पीतै *pítai*.	पीता *pítá*.

* Or पीअलौं *píalõ*, and so throughout.
† Or पीअबौं *píabõ*, and so throughout.

CONDITIONAL MOOD.

Person.	Present.		Preterite.	
	Singular.	Plural.	Singular.	Plural.
1st	पीऊँ *píú*.	पी *pí*.	पीतौं *pítõ*.	पीती *píti*.
2nd	पीवेँ *píwẽ*.	पीअ *pía*.	पीतेँ *pítẽ*.	पीतऽ *píta*.
3rd	पीवै *píwai*.	पीवैन्ह *píwainh*.	पिबैत *pibait*.	पीता *pítá*.

§ 91. **Example of a verb whose root ends in ऊ ú:—**

√चू *chú*, 'drip.'

INFINITIVE (2ND FORM): चूअल *chúal*, 'to drip.'

PRES. PART. चुऐत *chuait.*

INDICATIVE MOOD.

Person.	Preterite.		Future.	
	Singular.	Plural.	Singular.	Plural.
1st	चूलों *chúlõ.*	चूली *chúli.*	चूबों *chúbõ.*	चूअब *chúab.*
2nd	चूलैं *chúlẽ.*	चूलठ *chúla.*	चूबैं *chúbẽ.*	चूबठ *chúba.*
3rd	चूअल *chúal.*	चूला *chúlá.*	चूतै *chútai.*	चूता *chútá.*

CONDITIONAL MOOD.

Person.	Present.		Preterite.	
	Singular.	Plural.	Singular.	Plural.
1st	चूऊँ *chúú.*	चूई *chúí.*	चूतों* *chútõ.*	चूती *chúti.*
2nd	चूएँ *chúẽ.*	चूअ *chúa.*	चूतैं *chútẽ.*	चूतठ *chúta.*
3rd	चूऐ *chúai.*	चूऐन्ह *chúainh*	चुऐत *chuait.*	चूता *chútá.*

* Or चूइतों *chuitõ*, and so on throughout.

§ 92. Example of a verb whose root ends in ओ *o*:—

√ रो *ro*, 'weep.'

INFINITIVE (2ND FORM): रोअल *roal*, 'to weep.'
PRES. PART. रोइत *roït* or रोऐत *rŏait*.

INDICATIVE MOOD.

Person.	PRETERITE.		FUTURE.	
	Singular.	Plural.	Singular.	Plural.
1st	रोअलौं *roälõ*.*	रोअली *roäli*.	रोअबौं *roäbõ*.†	रोअब *roäb*.
2nd	रोअलें *roälẽ*.	रोअलह *roäla*.	रोअबें *roäbẽ*.	रोअबह *roäba*.
3rd	रोअल *roäl*.	रोअला *roälá*.	रोतै *rotai*.	रोअता *roätá*.

* Or रोलौं *rolõ*, and so throughout.
† रोबौं *robõ*, and so throughout the first and second persons.

CONDITIONAL MOOD.

Person.	PRESENT.		PRETERITE.	
	Singular.	Plural.	Singular.	Plural.
1st	रोऊँ *roû*.	रोई *roi*.	रोइतौं *roïtõ*.*	रोइती *roïti*.
2nd	रोएँ *roẽ*.	रोअ *roa*.	रोइतें *roïtẽ*.	रोइतह *roïta*.
3rd	रोऐ *roai*.	रोऐन्ह *roainh*.	रोऐत *rŏait*.	रोइता *roïtá*.

* Or रोअतौं *roätõ*, or रोतौं *rotõ*, and so throughout.

For further examples of verbs of this class, see conjugation of √ हो *ho*, § 53 & ff. This root √ रो *ro* is not much used in Southern Maithilí, the √ कान *kán* being preferred. It is, however, given as an example for the sake of uniformity with the other grammars of this series.

CHAPTER IX.

IRREGULAR VERBS.

§ 93. The following verbs are irregular only in their preterite tense indicative :— √ कर *kar*, 'do ;' √ धर *dhar*, 'seize' or 'place ;' √ मर *mar*, 'die ;' √ हो *ho*, 'become ;' and √ जा *já*, 'go.' The conjugation of √ कर *kar* and √ जा *já* is therefore given in that tense only. √ धर *dhar* and √ मर *mar* are conjugated exactly like √ कर *kar*, and are therefore not given. Besides, the irregular forms √ कर *kar*, √ धर *dhar*, and √ मर *mar*, have also each a regular form of the preterite indicative.

The conjugation of √ हो *ho* has been already given in § 53 and ff., and is not given here.

The verbs √ दे *de*, 'give,' and √ ले *le*, 'take,' are more or less irregular throughout all tenses, especially the preterite indicative and present conditional. The verb √ दे *de* is therefore given conjugated throughout the four radical and participial tenses. The verb √ ले *le* is conjugated precisely like the verb √ दे *de*.

§ 94. √ कर *kar*, 'do.'

INFINITIVE (2ND FORM) : { करल *karal*, कैल *kail*,
करल *kaïl* or कएल *kaël*.

PRES. PART. करैत *karait*.
PAST PART. करल *karal*, कैल *kail*, करल *kaïl*, or कएल *kaël*.

√ धर *dhar*, 'seize,' 'place.'

INFINITIVE (2ND FORM) : { धरल *dharal*, धैल *dhail*,
धरल *dhaïl*, or धएल *dhaël*.

PRES. PART. धरैत *dharait*.

PAST PART. धरल *dharal*, धैल *dhail*, धरल *dhaïl*, or धएल *dhaël*.

INDICATIVE MOOD.

Person.	Irregular Preterite.		Regular Preterite.	
	Singular.	Plural.	Singular.	Plural.
1st	कैलों *kailŏ.**	कैली *kailī.*	करलों *kar'lŏ.*	करली *kar'lī.*
2nd	कैलें *kailĕ.*	कैलह *kaila.*	करलें *kar'lĕ.*	करलह *kar'la.*
3rd	कैलन्कै *kail'kai.*	कैलन्का *kail'ká.*	करलन्कै *karal'kai.*	करलन्का *karal'ká.*

* Or कइलों *kaïlŏ* or कएलों *kaĕlŏ,* and so throughout.

The following forms of the conjunctive participle should be noted:— कह कह *ka ka* or कै कह *kai ka,* 'having done.'

Similarly is conjugated √ धर *dhar* (धैलों *dhailŏ,* धरलों *dhar'lŏ,* &c.)

§ 95. √ मर *mar,* 'die.'

VERBAL NOUN (2ND FORM): मरल *maral* or मैल *mail;* also मुअल *mual.*
PRES. PART. „ मरैत *marait.*
PAST PART. „ मरल *maral* or मैल *mail.*

PRETERITE INDICATIVE.

Conjugated exactly like √ कर *kar,* above: thus मैलों *mailŏ,* मरलों *mar'lŏ,* &c. The preterite may also be मुअलों *mualŏ,* &c.

§ 96. √जा *já*, 'go.'

This root is conjugated like √खा *khá* in all tenses but the preterite indicative, which is therefore here given. (See § 87 and ff.) With it is given the same tense of √आ *á*, 'come,' for the sake of comparison.

VERBAL NOUN (2ND FORM) : आएल *áĕl*.	जाएल *jáĕl* or गेल *gel*.
PAST PART. आएल *áĕl*.	गेल *gel*.

Person.	√आ *á*, PRETERITE INDICATIVE.		√जा *já*, PRETERITE INDICATIVE.	
	Singular.	Plural.	Singular.	Plural.
1st	ऐलौं *ailõ*.	ऐली *ailĭ*.	गेलौं *gelõ*.*	गेली *gelĭ*.
2nd	ऐलें *ailẽ*.	ऐलह *aila*.	गेलें *gelẽ*.	गेलह *gela*.
3rd	आएल *áĕl*.	ऐला *ailá*.	गेल *gel*.	गेला *gelá*.

* Or गैलौं *gailõ*, and so throughout.

§ 97. √दे *de*, 'give.'

VERBAL NOUN (2ND FORM) : देल *del*, 'to give.'

PRES. PART. देत *dait*.

PAST PART. देल *del*.

INDICATIVE MOOD.

Person.	PRETERITE.		FUTURE.	
	Singular.	Plural.	Singular.	Plural.
1st	देलौं *delõ*.	देली [illegible].	देबौं *debõ*.	देब *deb*.
2nd	देलें *delẽ*.	देलह *dela*.	देबें *debẽ*.	देबह *deba*.
3rd	देलन्कै *dĕl'kai*.	देलन्का *dĕl'ká*.	देतै *detai*.	देता *detá*.

CONDITIONAL MOOD.

Person.	PRESENT.		PRETERITE.	
	Singular.	Plural.	Singular.	Plural.
1st	देऊँ *deú* or दीयौं *díõ*.	दी *dí*.	देतौं *detõ*.*	देती *deti*.
2nd	दे *de*, देँ *dẽ*, दै *dai*, दैँ *daĩ*.	दठ *da*.	देतेँ *detẽ*.	देतठ *deta*.
3rd	दै *dai*, दीऐ *díai*.	देथ *deth* or दैन्ह *dainh*.	देइत *deït* or दैत *dait*.	देता *detá*.

* Or दैतौं *daitõ*, and so throughout.

PRECATIVE : दीहौ *díhau*, दीही *díhí*.

Similarly is conjugated the √ ले *le*, 'take,' the letter ल *la* being substituted for the letter द *da* throughout.

CHAPTER X.

THE PASSIVE VERB.

§ 98. The passive verb is formed by conjugating the verbal noun ending in अल *al* with the verb √ जा *já*, 'go:' thus देखल जाएल *dekhal jáĕl*, 'to be seen.' This verbal noun is not altered for gender, number, person, or tense, only the verb जाएल *jáĕl* being conjugated. Thus—

Indicative Preterite Masculine : '*I was seen,' &c.*

Person.	Singular.	Plural.
1st	देखल गेलौं *dekhal gelŏ.*	देखल गेली *dekhal gelí.*
2nd	देखल गेलेँ *dekhal gelĕ.*	देखल गेलह *dekhal gela.*
3rd	देखल गेल *dekhal gel.*	देखल गेला *dekhal gelá.*

§ 99. This verbal noun in अल *al* must be carefully distinguished from the past participle having the same termination. The former even in irregular verbs is sometimes quite regular, so that we have verbal nouns such as जाएल *jáĕl,* besides past participles like गेल *gel.* At the same time it must be remembered that the verbal noun can also take the form of the past participle as well as its proper form: so that we may have गेल *gel* as a verbal noun as well as जाएल *jáĕl.* An example of an irregular passive verb is जाएल जाइछै *jáĕl jáïchhai* (impersonal), 'it is gone'—*itum est*; but, used in the sense of the potential, 'it can go.' When neuter verbs are used in the passive voice, they are always used in an impersonal potential sense: thus, हमरा से जाएल नह जाइछै *ham'rá se jáĕl na jáïchhai*, 'by me it cannot be gone,' *i.e.* 'I cannot go.'

§ 100. Another common form of the passive is made by adding to the direct form of the first variety of the verbal noun (which is the same in form as the root) the verb परल *paral*, 'to fall;' the whole then forms an intensive compound. (See § 114.)

Examples of this form are—

किछु किछु जान परैयऽ *kichhu kichhu ján paraiya*, 'a little is evident,' *i.e.* 'it is slightly apparent.'

एकरा से ई बूझ परैयऽ *ĕk'rá se í bújh paraiya*, 'from this, this is understood.'

कुड़्मड़ नहिँ देख परैछै *kuṛ'mar nahĩ dekh paraichhai*, 'it is not seen to be at all increased in size.'

§ 101. The Potential Passive Voice.

This voice is formed by adding आ *á* to the root: thus √ देख *dekh* potential passive देखा *dekhá*. देखा *dekhá* is then conjugated exactly like any intransitive verb in आ *á*, as explained in § 88. It thus differs from the causal verb (see § 103), when it adds आव *áw* to the root. The potential passive is conjugated quite regularly, the following being its principal parts, with which the corresponding causal forms are given for the sake of comparison.

	POTENTIAL PASSIVE.	CAUSAL.
Root	देखा *dekhá.*	देखाव *dĕkháw.*
Infinitive, 2nd form ...	देखाएल *dĕkháĕl* ; obl. देखैला *dĕkhailá.*	देखावल *dĕkháwal* ; obl. देखौला *dĕkhaulá.*
Past part. ...	देखाएल *dĕkháĕl.*	देखावल *dĕkháwal.*
1st pl. pret. ind. ...	देखैली *dĕkhailí.*	देखौली *dĕkhaulí.*
2nd sing. pret. ind. ...	देखैलेँ *dĕkhailẽ.*	देखौलेँ *dĕkhaulẽ.*
2nd pl. pret. ind. ...	देखैलऽ *dĕkhaila.*	देखौलऽ *dĕkhaula.*
3rd sing. pret. ind. ...	देखाएल *dĕkháĕl.*	देखौलक *dĕkhaulak.*
3rd pl. pret. ind. ...	देखैला *dĕkhailá.*	देखौलन्का *dĕkhaŭl'ká.*

It will be observed that the potential passive verb shortens its antepenultimate, as occurs in the case of causals. (See § 104.)

There is a tendency, which amounts almost to a rule, to drop the junction vowel in the conjugation of the tenses not derived from the past participle of the potential passive; and, moreover, in the forms derived from the present participle, even to drop the final आ *á* of the root, substituting instead the letter अ *a*, which is pronounced quite fully, thus differing from the similarly spelt preterite conjunctive of the simple verb (§ 63). Thus we get the following forms:—

	Usual forms, dropping the junction vowel.	Regular forms, according to § 89.
Infinitive, 3rd form	देखाब *dĕkháb.*	देखाएब *dĕkháĕb.*
1st pl. fut. ...	देखाब *dĕkháb.*	देखाएब *dĕkháĕb*
2nd pl. fut. ...	देखाबह *dĕkhába.*	देखैबह *dĕkhaiba.*
3rd sg. fut. ...	देखातै *dĕkhátai* or देखतै *dĕkhatai*, (but 2nd sing. pret. conj. of simple verb, देख्तै *dĕkh'tai.*)	देखैतै *dĕkhaitai.*
1st pl. pret. conj. ...	देखाती *dĕkháti* or देखती [*dekhati.*	देखैती *dĕkhaiti.*
3rd pret. conj. and pres. part.	देखात *dĕkhát* or देखत *dekhat.*	देखाइत *dĕkháït.*

The potential passive has a peculiar force, intimating, not that a thing *is* done, but that it *can be* done. Thus ई पोथी पढ़ाइयह *i pothi paṛháïya*, 'this book *can be* read,' but ई पोथी पढ़ल जाइयह *i pothí paṛhal jáïya*, 'this book is being read.' For further examples of this passive, see § 103.

§ 102. The Periphrastic Passive Voice.

A very common kind of passive voice is formed by placing the verb √ आ *á* after the first or shortest form of a verbal noun in the locative case: thus देखे मेँ आएल *dekhĕ mẽ áĕl*, 'the coming into seeing,' *i.e.* 'to be seen.' The person by whom the action is done is put in the oblique genitive form of the noun or pronoun when there is one: thus तोँ हमरा देखे मेँ ऐलऽ *tõ ham'rá dekhĕ mẽ aila*, 'you came into my seeing,' 'you were seen by me.' The following example shows a verb in this voice conjugated in the present indicative masculine:—

Singular.	Plural.
1. देखे मेँ अवैछौँ *dekhĕ mẽ awaichhaũ.*	1. देखे मेँ अवैछी *dekhĕ mẽ awaichhí.*
2. देखे मेँ अवैछेँ *dekhĕ mẽ awaichhẽ.*	2. देखे मेँ अवैछऽ *dekhĕ mẽ awaichha.*
3. देखे मेँ अवैयऽ *dekhĕ mẽ awaiya.*	3. देखे मेँ अवैछैन्ह *dekhĕ mẽ awaichhainh.*

EXAMPLE.—हमरा सभ तोहरा देखे मेँ अवैछी *ham'rá sabh tõh'rá dekhĕ mẽ awaichhí*, 'we are seen by you.'

CHAPTER XI.

CAUSAL VERBS.

§ 103. A causal verb is formed by adding आव *áw* to the root of the simple verb, and a double causal by adding वाव *wáw*. The stems thus formed are conjugated exactly like verbs whose roots end in आव *áw*. (See § 87.) The long vowel of आव *áw* and वाव *wáw* is, as usual, liable to be shortened in the antepenultimate (see General Introduction, § 36); and if the व *wa* is followed by the neutral vowel, it becomes उ *u* (see General Introduction, § 37), which with a preceding अ *a* (see General Introduction, § 35) may be written औ *au*. In Madhepúrá (and optionally elsewhere), however, आ *á* and वा *wá* are added instead of आव *áw* and वाव *wáw*, and then the verb takes the junction vowel इ *i* instead of उ *u*. See § 87 and ff.

Thus, taking the simple verb √ उठ *uṭh*, 'rise,' the first plural definite present indicative of its causal would be regularly उठ्वैछी *uṭh'waichhí*. But the first plural preterite would be उठवल्ही *uṭhaw'lí*, which (as व *wa* is followed by the neutral vowel) becomes (General Introduction, § 37) उठउली *uṭhaülí* or उठौली *uṭhaulí*. In Madhepúrá (and optionally elsewhere), these words would be उठाइछी *uṭháichhí* and उठैली *uṭhailí* respectively.

Similarly, for the double causal the forms would be उठ्ववैछी *uṭh'wawaichhí* and उठ्वउली *uṭh'waülí*, or उठ्वौली *uṭh'waulí*. In Madhepúrá (and optionally elsewhere) these words would be उठ्वाइछी *uṭh'wáichhí* and उठ्वैली *uṭh'wailí* respectively.

It will thus be seen that the causal may either be the same in form as the potential passive (§ 101), or may take ओ *ŏ* as a junction vowel, which the potential passive never does. Examples are—

Potential Passive.—तोँ देखैलह, आर हम परा गेली, *tŏ dĕkhaila, ăur ham pará gelí*, 'you became visible, and I ran away.'

Causal.—तोँ एखन्नी तक हमरा ब्याकरन नहिँ देखैलह (or देखौलह) *tŏ ĕkh'ni tak ham'rá byákaran nahĩ dĕkhaila* (or *dĕkhaula*), 'you have not yet shown me the grammar.'

Potential Passive.—जनि जाइत हो, तोँ देखाबै *jani jäit ho; tŏ dĕkhábai*, 'don't be going; you will be liable to be seen.'

Causal.—तोँ देखाबै हम॰रा, हम देखाबौँ तोह॰रा *tŏ dĕkhábai ham'rá, ham dĕkhábaŭ tŏh'rá*, 'you will show me; I shall show you.'

Potential Passive or Causal.—ऊ ओने बाटे त॰ जाइछै, परन्तु देखतै *ú onĕ báte ta jäichhai, parantu dĕkhatai*, 'he is going by that way, but he will be seen;' or, 'he is going by that way, but he will show.'

Simple verb, 2nd preterite conjunctive.—तोँ जे देख॰तै, त॰ ले लितै *tŏ je dĕkh'tai, ta le litai*, 'had you seen, you would have taken it.'

The following are examples of the regular formation of causals and double causals. In Madhepúrá the final व *w* of the causal and double causal must be omitted, and this may also be optionally done elsewhere:—

Simple Verb.	Causal.	Double Causal.
उठ *uṭh*, 'rise.'	उठाव *uṭháw*, 'raise.'	उठ॰वाव *uṭh'wáw*, 'cause to raise.'
कह *kah*, 'say.'	कहाव *kaháw*, 'cause to speak.'	कह॰वाव *kah'wáw*, 'cause to cause to speak.'
झप *jhap*, 'be hidden.'	झपाव *jhapáw*, 'hide.'	झप॰वाव *jhap'wáw*, 'cause to hide.'
पक *pak*, 'be cooked.'	पकाव *pakáw*, 'cook.'	पक॰वाव *pak'wáw*, 'cause to cook.'
मर॰म *marm*, 'be turned.'	मर॰माव *mar'máw*, 'turn.'	मरम॰वाव *maram'wáw*, 'cause to turn.'
मिल *mil*, 'meet.'	मिलाव *miláw*, 'mix.'	मिल॰वाव *mil'wáw*, 'cause to mix.'
लुक *luk*, 'be hidden.'	लुकाव *lukáw*, 'hide.'	लुक॰वाव *luk'wáw*, 'cause to hide.'
सुन *sun*, 'hear.'	सुनाव *sunáw*, 'tell.'	सुन॰वाव *sun'wáw*, 'cause to tell.'

§ 104. If the simple root contains a long vowel it is shortened, viz. आ *á* to अ *a*, ई *í* to इ *i*, ऊ *ú* to उ *u*, ए *e* to ऎ *ĕ*, ओ *o* to ऒ *ŏ*, ऐ *ai* to ऐ *aĭ*, and औ *au* to औ *aŭ*.

Similarly, if a root ends in a double consonant, it is made single: thus—

Simple Verb.	Causal.	Double Causal.
√ जाग *jág*, 'be awake.'	जगाव *jagáw*, 'awaken.'	जगन्वाव *jag'wáw*, 'cause to awake.'
√ पाक *pák*, 'be cooked.'	पकाव *pakáw*, 'cook.'	पकन्वाव *pak'wáw*, 'cause to cook.'
√ जीत *jít*, 'conquer.'	जिताव *jitáw*, 'cause to conquer.'	जितन्वाव *jit'wáw*, 'cause to cause to conquer.'
√ सीख *síkh*, 'learn.'	सिखाव *sikháw*, 'teach.'	सिखन्वाव *sikh'wáw*, 'cause to teach.'
√ पी *pí*, 'drink.'	पिआव *piáw*, 'cause to drink.'	पिअवाव *piawáw*, 'cause to cause to drink.'
√ तीत *tít*, 'be wet.'	तिताव *titáw*, 'moisten.'	तितन्वाव *tit'wáw*, 'cause to moisten.'
√ घूम *ghúm*, 'be turned.'	घुमाव *ghumáw*, 'turn.'	घुमन्वाव *ghum'wáw*, 'cause to turn.'
√ बूड़ *búṛ*, 'sink.'	बुड़ाव *buṛáw*, 'immerse.'	बुड़न्वाव *buṛ'wáw*, 'cause to immerse.'
√ सूत *sút*, 'sleep.'	सुताव *sutáw*, 'put to sleep.'	सुतन्वाव *sut'wáw*, 'cause to put to sleep.'
√ देख *dekh*, 'see.'	देखाव *dĕkháw*, 'show.'	देखन्वाव *dĕkh'wáw*, 'cause to show.'
√ हेल *hel*, 'swim.'	हेलाव *hĕláw*, 'cause to swim.'	हेलन्वाव *hĕl'wáw*, 'cause to cause to swim.'
√ बैस *bais*, 'sit.'	बैसाव *baĭsáw*, 'seat.'	बैसन्वाव *baĭs'wáw*, 'cause to sit.'
√ दौग *daug*, 'run.'	दौगाव *daŭgáw*, 'cause to run.'	दौगन्वाव *daŭg'wáw*, 'cause to cause to run.'
√ लुक्क *lukk*, 'be hidden.'	लुकाव *lukáw*, 'hide.'	लुकन्वाव *luk'wáw*, 'cause to hide.'

Note in connection with the above :—

Simple Verb.	Causal.
√ देख *dekh*, 'see'	देखन्लाव *děkh'láw*, also regular.
√ कह *kah*, 'speak'.........	कहन्लाव *kah'láw*, also regular.
√ खा *khá*, 'eat'	खिआव *khiáw*.
√ पी *pí*, 'drink'	पिलाव *piláw*, also regular.

§ 105. Some primitive neuter verbs, having a monosyllabic root enclosing a short vowel, form the first causal by simply lengthening that vowel. The double causal is formed in the usual way, *e.g.*—

Simple Verb.	Causal.
√ कट *kaṭ*, 'be cut'	काट *káṭ*, 'cut.'
√ बन्ह *banh*, 'be tied'	बान्ह *bánh*, 'tie.'
√ लद *lad*, 'be loaded'	लाद *lád*, 'load.'
√ खिंच *khiṅch*, 'be dragged'	खींच* *khích*, 'drag.'

§ 106. Sometimes a cognate diphthong is substituted for the long vowel, *e.g.*—

खुल *khul*, 'be open.'	खोल *khol*, 'open.'
घुर *ghur*, 'melt.' (*Neut.*)	घोर *ghor*, 'melt.' (*Act.*)

§ 107. The verb √ निकस *nikas*, 'come out,' makes its causal निकास *nikás*, 'take out,' on the analogy of the above. So also √ पसर *pasar*, 'be scattered,' makes पसार *pasár*, 'scatter,' 'extend;' √ ससर *sasar*, 'slip,' ससार *sasár*, 'cause to slip;' √ उपर *upar*, 'be rooted up,' उपार *upár*, 'root up;' and √ उखर *ukhar*, 'be rooted up,' उखार *ukhár*, 'root up.'

* When the vowel is lengthened, *anuswár* becomes *anunásik*. (Compare General Introduction, § 28.)

§ 108. The following are irregular :—

Simple Verb.	Causal.	Double Causal.
√ अट *aṭ*, 'be stopped.'	आर *ár*, 'stop.'	अराव *aráw*.
√ फट *phaṭ* or फाट *pháṭ*, 'be torn.'	फार *phár*, 'tear,'	फराव *pharáw*.
√ छूट *chhúṭ*, 'be separated.'	छोर *chhor* or छार *chhár*, 'separate.'	छोराव *chhŏráw*.
√ जूट *júṭ*, 'be joined.'	जोर *jor*, 'join.'	जोराव *jŏráw*.
√ टूट *ṭúṭ*, 'be broken.'	तोर *tor*, 'break.'	तोराव *tŏráw*,
√ फूट *phúṭ*, 'be burst.'	फोर *phor*, 'burst.'	फोराव *phŏráw*.
√ बिक्क *bikk*, 'be sold.'	बेँच *bēch* or बिकाव *bikáw*, 'sell.'	बेँचाव *bĕcháw*.
√ रह *rah*, 'remain.'	राख *rákh* or रक्ख *rakkh*, 'place.'	रखाव *rakháw*.
√ मर *mar*, 'die.'	मार *már* or मुआव *muáw*, 'cause to die.'	

CHAPTER XII.

COMPOUND VERBS.

§ 109. Compound verbs are either intensives, potentials, completives, frequentatives, desideratives, continuatives, staticals, inceptives, permissives, or acquisitives.

§ 110. Compound verbs may be classed as—(1) those formed with the verbal noun, and (2) those formed with the participles.

(1) Those formed with the verbal noun are—

a) Intensives.
b) Potentials.
c) Completives.
d) Frequentatives.
e) Desideratives.
f) Inceptives.
g) Permissives.
h) Acquisitives.

(2) Those formed with the participles—

a) Continuatives.
b) Staticals.

Class I.—Compounds formed with the Verbal Noun.*

§ 111. There are three varieties of the verbal noun—

a) In अ *a* (silent) or इ *i*, oblique form ए *ĕ*, ऐ *aĭ*, or अ *a*; as देख *dekh* or देखि *dekhi*, obl. देखे *dekhĕ*, देखैं *dekhaĭ*, or देखअ *dekha.*

b) In अल *al*, oblique form ्ला *'lá*; as देखल *dekhal*, obl. देख्ला *dĕkh'lá.*

c) In अब *ab*, oblique form ्बा *'bá*; as देखब *dekhab*, obl. देख्बा *dĕkh'bá.*

The direct first form in अ *a* (silent) is always the same as the root.

Compound verbs are either formed with the direct form of the first, second, or third variety of the verbal noun, or with the oblique form of the first variety.

---

* Much of the succeeding matter is based on Kellogg's Hindí Grammar.

§ 112. *Intensives, Potentials,* and *Completives,* are generally formed with the direct form of the first variety; *Frequentatives* and *Desideratives* are generally formed with the direct form of the second variety; *Inceptives, Permissives,* and *Acquisitives,* are always formed with the oblique form of the first variety.

§ 113. *Intensive* compounds intensify or otherwise modify the meaning of the verb whose root stands first in the compound. They are formed by adding to a verbal noun of the first variety in the direct form one of certain other verbs, which latter verb in conjunction with the verbal noun is then conjugated as usual. This second conjugated member does not, however, retain its separate character and significance, but only modifies, in accordance with the general idea which it embodies, the meaning of the unconjugated verbal noun to which it is annexed. Examples are—

फेँकल *phĕkal,* 'to throw.'	फेँक (or फेँकि) देल *phĕk* (or *phĕki*) *del,* 'to throw away.'
तोरल *toral,* 'to break.'	तोर डालल *tor ḍálal,* 'to break in pieces.'
बनल *banal,* 'to be made.'	बन आएल *ban áĕl* or बन जाएल *ban jáĕl,* 'to be completed.'
खाएल *kháĕl,* 'to eat.'	खा जाएल *khá jáĕl,* 'to eat up.'
बोलल *bolal,* 'to speak.'	बोल उठल *bol uṭhal,* 'to speak suddenly.'
काटल *káṭal,* 'to cut.'	काट लेल *káṭ lel,* 'to cut for oneself.'
राखल *rákhal,* 'to place.'	राख लेल *rákh lel,* 'to lay by.'

§ 114. The auxiliary verbs usually employed to form intensives are—

देल	*del,*	'to give,'	implying *intensity.*
डालल	*ḍálal,*	'to throw,'	" *violence.*
आएल	*áĕl,*	'to come,'	" *completion.*
जाएल	*jáĕl,*	'to go,'	" *completion.*
परल	*paral,*	'to fall,'	" *chance.*
उठल	*uṭhal,*	'to rise,'	" *suddenness.*
लेल	*lel,*	'to take,'	" *reflexiveness.*

परल *paral* is also used in intensive compounds to form passives of transitive verbs. (See § 100.)

§ 115. *Potentials* are formed by adding to the same form of the verbal noun of any verb the verb सकल *sakal*, 'to be able,' which may then be conjugated throughout. Examples are—

बोलि सकब *boli sakab*, 'to be able to speak.'

ऊ दौग सकैछै *ú daug sakaichhai*, 'he can run.'

हम जाइ सकऽबै *ham jáï sak'bai*, 'I shall be able to go.'

हमें नहिं जाइ सकैछी *hamẽ nahĩ jáï sakaichhí*, 'I cannot go.'

Sometimes the oblique instead of the direct form of the verbal noun is used, *e.g.* ऊ दौगें सकैछै *ú daugẽ sakaichhai*, instead of the second example above.

§ 116. *Completives* are formed by adding to the same form of the verbal noun of a verb the verb चुकल *chukal*, 'to be finished,' which may then be conjugated throughout. This compound denotes the *completion* of the act denoted by the primary member of the compound. Examples are—

ऊ खाइ चुकल *ú kháï chukal*, 'he has done eating.'

जब ऊ खाइ चुकऽतै *jab ú kháï chuk'tai*, 'when he shall have eaten.'

ऊ तऽ जाइ चुकऽलै *ú ta jáï chuk'lai*, 'he is indeed already gone.'

Sometimes the direct form of the second variety of the verbal noun is used: thus, ऊ खाएल चुकऽलै *ú kháël chuk'lai*, 'he has done eating.'

§ 117. *Frequentatives* are formed by affixing to the direct form of the second variety of the verbal noun of any verb the verb करल *karal*, 'to do,' which may then be used in any tense. Examples are—

आएल करऽ *áël kara*, 'come often,' *lit.* 'do the act of coming.'

हमें शास्त्र के पढ़ल करैछी *hamẽ sástr ke paṛhal karaichhí*, 'I am in the habit of reading the shástras.'

तोहें हमर बात सभ मानल करऽ *tohẽ hamar bát sabh mánal kara*, 'always obey my words.'

तोहें कहिने ऐसन करल करैछऽ *tohẽ kahine aisan karal karaichha*, 'why do you always do so?'

ऊ जाएल करैछै *ú jáël karaichhai*, 'he often goes.'

Sometimes the direct form of the third variety of the verbal noun is used: thus, ऊ बाजब करैछै *ú bájab karaichhai*, 'he speaks frequently.'

§ 118. *Desideratives* are formed, like frequentatives, with the direct form of the verbal noun in अल *al,* substituting the verb चाहल *cháhal,* 'to wish,' for करल *karal* as the second or conjugated member. They denote primarily *desire* to do the action expressed of the principal member; secondarily, the *immediate futurity* of that action. An example is—

ऊ बाजल चहैछै *ú bájal chahaichhai,* 'he wishes to speak.'

Sometimes the principal verb is put in the oblique form of the first variety of the verbal noun with or without the dative postposition के *ke* or ला *lá,* लेल *lel.* This is the more usual form in South Darbhangá. Examples are—

ऊ बोलॆ ला चहैछै *ú bolĕ lá chahaichhai,* 'he wishes to speak.'

घड़ी बाजे (or बाजे लेल) चहैछै *ghaṛí bájĕ* (or *bájĕ lel*) *chahaichhai,* 'the clock is about to strike.'

ऊ जाए ला चहैछै *ú jáĕ lá chahaichhai,* 'he wishes to go.'

ऊ मरै चहैछै *ú maraĭ chahaichhai,* 'he is about to die.'

The desiderative compound in the precative form is idiomatically used to express obligation or duty. Examples are—

ई पोथी के पढ़ै चाही *ĭ pothĭ ke paṛhaĭ cháhí,* '(one) ought to read this book.' (*Lit.* 'be good enough to wish to read.')

तोहरा उहाँ जाए के चाही *tŏh'rá uhā̆ jáĕ ke cháhĭ,* 'it is right for you (*i.e.* you ought) to go there.'

§ 119. *Inceptives* are formed by using the inflected form of the first variety of the verbal noun in construction with the verb लागल *lágal,* 'to be joined,' 'to begin,' and denote the action of the verbal noun as *beginning.* Examples are—

कहै लगल्है *kahaĭ lag'lai,* 'he began to say.'

मारे लगल्है *márĕ lag'lai,* 'he began to beat.'

बाघ खाए लगल्है *bágh kháĕ lag'lai,* 'the tiger began to eat.'

§ 120. *Permissives* are formed by combining the same form of the verbal noun with the verb देब *del*, 'to give,' and express *permission* to do the act denoted by the verbal noun. Examples are—

हमऽरा जाए दऽ *ham'rá jáě da*, 'let me go.'

हमऽरा के बोलै दऽ *ham'rá ke bolaĭ da*, 'be good enough to let me speak.'

ऊ ओकऽरा खाए देलऽकै *ú ŏk'rá kháě děl'kai*, 'he allowed him to eat.'

§ 121. *Acquisitives* are the exact converse of the preceding, and are formed in the same way, substituting पावब *páwal*, 'to get,' for देब *del*. Examples are—

तोहेँ उहाँ जाए नैं पैबऽ *tohĕ uhá jáě naĭ paiba*, 'you will not obtain permission to go there.'

हमेँ बैसे नैं पौलौं *hamĕ baisě naĭ paulaŭ*, 'I was not allowed to sit.'

Class II.—Compounds formed from the Participles.

§ 122. *Continuatives* are formed by combining the present or past participle of any verb with the verbs जाएब *jáěl*, 'to go,' or रहब *rahal*, 'to remain.' The participle may be either in the direct or oblique form. It must be remembered that in the case of neuter verbs the oblique form is the same as the direct: thus, गिरब *giral*, obl. गिरब *giral*; while in the case of active verbs, it is formed by adding ए *e* or अ *a*: thus, देखब *dekhal*, obl. देखऽले *děkh'le* or देखऽलऽ *děkh'la*. The present participle always has its oblique form in ते *te* or तऽ *ta*, both in active and neuter verbs: thus, देखैत *děkhait*, obl. देखऽते *děkh'te* or देखऽतऽ *děkh'ta*; गिरैत *girait*, obl. गिरऽते *gir'te* or गिरऽतऽ *gir'ta*.

The compound with जाएब *jáěl* expresses *steady progression*, and with रहब *rahal* the *continuance* of a complete action. Examples—

ऊ लिखऽते जाइछै *ú likh'te jáichhai*, 'he is going on writing.'

ऊ सभ लरऽकी पढ़ैत जाइरहे *ú sabh lar'kí parhait jáirahe*, 'those girls were going on reading.'

पानी बहल जाइयछ *páni bahal jáiya*, 'the water keeps flowing away.'

ऊ गबैत रहैछै *ú gawait rahaichhai*, 'she continues singing.'

नदी के धार बहैत रहैछै *nadí kĕ dhár bahait rahaichhai*, 'the stream of the river keeps flowing on.'

तोहें किये हसैत रहैछह *tohẽ kiye hasait rahaichha*, 'why do you keep laughing?'

Closely connected with the above is a common combination in which the past participle in its direct form takes the first place and a verb of motion the second place. An example is—

एक बाघ परल फिरैछै *ĕk bágh paral phiraichhai*, 'a tiger is prowling about.'

नौंड़ी चलल जाइरहे *nãũṛí chalal jáirahe*, 'the girl was going along.'

§ 123. *Staticals* denote motion in a state of doing anything. They are formed by combining a verb of motion with a present or past participle. Examples are—

ऊ कनैत (or कानल) अबैछै *ú kanait* (or *kánal*) *awaichhai*, 'he comes weeping.'

एक मौगी गबैत अबैत रहे *ĕk maugí gawait await rahe*, 'a woman was coming singing.'

DIVISION III.

INDECLINABLES.

§ 124. See General Introduction.

APPENDIX.

THE following selections are in the dialect of the Begú Sarái subdivision of North Munger. The conversation and fables were translated for me by Bhattan Lál, Guru of Nur'púr, in that subdivision. An English translation of them and of the conversation will be found in the General Introduction.

SELECTIONS IN THE SOUTH MAITHILÍ DIALECT.

CONVERSATION BETWEEN TWO VILLAGERS.

१ प्रश्न कहौ भाइ, कहाँ से अवैछौ ?

उत्तर परन्सौया गाँव से अवैछी ।

२ प्र. अहाँ से कौन चलन्लौँ रहे * ?

उ. सबेरे केर चलल छिकौँ ।

३ प्र. केथी लेल अहाँ गेलौँ रहे ?

उ. अहाँ हमर खेत थेछ, ओकन्रा देखै लेल गेलौँ रहे ।

४ प्र. ओहि मेँ की बुनलाँ थेछ ?

उ. खाली रहरि बुनल गेलै थछ ।

५ प्र. कहौ भाइ, अबन्की फसिल केर की रङ्ग छै ?

उ. ई फसिल केर की हाल पुछैछै, पानि बरन्सै बिना बड़ बिगरन्ला भेल ।

६ प्र. आइ काल्ह आरस केर भाइ कै नहिँ देखैछिऐन्ह ।

उ. हमर भाइ आइ काल्ह किला मेँ नोकर छन ; हनी बड़त काम अवैछन ।

---

* First person used honorifically for the second person. See § 41.

७ प्र. आइस कोर बड़की गाय कोर की हाल छेन ?

उ. ऊ आइ काल्ह गाभिन छेन, मुदा अहार नहिँ मिलला से टूट गेल छेन।

८ प्र. कै महिना से गाभिन छठ ?

उ. हे ते आठ मास से मुदा पेट ओकर कुड़लड़ * नहिँ देख परैछे।

९ प्र. लँबबेछौ कि नहिँ छौ ?

उ. हँ, किछु किछु जान परैछठ।

१० प्र. ई कै बियान होतै ? और कतै दूध देतै ?

उ. ई एकर आठम बियान छिकै। दू अढ़ाइ सेर दूध एक साँझ मेँ होएतै।

११ प्र. हमरा एक बकरी लेना † अछ ; आइस कोर छियाँ मोलत ?

उ. हमरा गाँव मेँ बकरी अबैछठ, मुदा दाम बहु छै।

१२ प्र. आइस कोर बकरी की भेल ?

उ. हमेँ घरे छेल ओकरा घोर पर झार देलौँ छठ।

१३ प्र. किछु दूध देछठ ?

उ. छरिका कोर पीऐ ओकर सो आइछै।

१४ प्र. एहोँ केतारी बुनलौँ छठ की नहिँ ?

उ. केतारी ते बुनलौँ छठ, मुदा ओकरा मेँ लाभ किछुव नहिँ छै।

१५ प्र. आइस कब नार मोठि मँगली मोल सकैछठ ?

उ. किया नहिँ ? पटौला पर ले लेछठ।

१६ प्र. आइस कन केतो मोठि अलेछक ?

उ. तीन मोठि ते माधलौँ अछ।

१७ प्र. आइस कोर आम कोर गाछी फरैछठ की नहिँ ?

उ. बकरी ते बढ़री लेल गाछ सभ मेँ लाही लाग गेलै ; नहिँ ते बहु होतै।

---

* When an animal is advanced in pregnancy, the swaying distended stomach is called by this name.

† See General Introduction, § 47.

१८ प्र. थोरि आम हमरौ अचार लेल देबठ ?

उ. जौन अहाँ केर जी चाहै, तौन तोरन्या लेबठ ।

१९ प्र. आइस केर लरिका किछु पढ़ैछन्ह कि नहिं ?

उ. हौँ, गुरु किहाँ आइयठ; अच्छर तै चिन्हल्लक, आइ काल्ह पहाड़ा पढ़ैयठ ।

२० प्र. इस्कूल मैं किय नहिं भेजैछी ?

उ. किछु सीख लै तब भेजब्बै ।

२१ प्र. हमहूँ * अपना लरिका कै अस्कोल मैं भेजै लेल चहैछी ?

उ. बेस ; तठ हमरा लरिका केर साथ ओकरौ † भेज देभौ ॥

FABLES.

पहिल बात ।

मुरगा आओर मोती केर दाना ।

एक मुरगा गोबर केर ढेर कै अङ्कुर से कोरैरहै । अचानक ओहि मैं से अरन्गौ मोती केर दाना निकसल्लै । मुरगा बाजल जे, बाह बाह कैसन रङ्ग रूप औ चमक कौत छिकै । ओकरौ एकरा पबैत, तौ फूल आइत, मुदा हमरा पेट केर छुधा एकरा सैं नहिं आइत । हाए, एगो चाउर के दाना हमैं पौतौं तब से मोती से बढ़ कै होइत । साँच बूझठ, जे अपना काम नठ आवे, से धूरह ममन्सार मैं परै ॥

दोसर बात ।

कँगाल के पुछन्नाइ आओर अतीथ के जबाब देनाइ ।

एगो कँगाल, कोइ पङ्चल अतीथ सैं पुछल्लक जे, हमैं भूखैं मरी आओर हमर परोँसिया गद्दी तकिया पर परल ओघन्राएल रहै, राति दीन चैन करै ; ओकरा मैं कौन गुन छै, जे दाता ओकरा मेहाँल कैलखिन्ह, आओर हमरा कँगाल बनौलन्का । ई सुन कै

---

* Emphatic for हमैं.

† Emphatic for ओकरा, 'him also.'

अतीथ जबाब देलन्कै ; जे, बाबा, तोँह इथीँ नहिँ सुन॰ले छठ जे, राम अपन बखख सभ केर परीक्षा लेथौ। जेकर जेहन कमाइ तेक॰रा तेहन देथौ ॥

तेसर बात।

देस पर॰देस फिर॰ला केर गुन।

कोइ भल मानुस एक गोसाँइ सँ कहल॰खिन्ह जे, महाराज जी, देस देस आओर गाँवे गाँव भटक॰ल फिर॰ला सँ की लाभ छौ। एक ठाम बैस कैँ पर॰मेसर मैँ लौँ किये नठ लग॰बैछठ आओर कोइ मख मैँ बैस कैँ दाता केर गुन किये नहिँ गबैछठ। जोगी जी कहल॰खिन्ह जे बाबा, ई बात सभ साँच है, मुदा तोँह ई कहावत नठ सुन॰ले है जे, बहतू पानि निर्मल, बान्हल पानि मैला होए। साधू जन चलैत घुमैत भला तथन्ही दाग नठ लागै कोइ।

चारिम बात ।

एक दीन जाड़ा के समे कोइ बरा आदिमी के घर मैँ आगि लग॰ले। सभ चीज जर के छाओर भे गेले। ज बाहर ठार हाथ मलैत रहथ, कि एक दुखिया परोसिया जारा से थर थर कँपैत घर सै निकस के हाथ सेँदे लागल। तब ज माल॰वाला बाजल : बाह जि बाह हेक॰री घर जरै कोइ तापे ॥

पाँचिम बात।

बान्हल लक॰री, आओर बिथ॰रल लक॰री।

एक किसान केर लरिका आपुस मैँ बर झराए झगरा करैत रहथ; कहि के बहुत समझौलक तैँओ कोइ किछु ने मन॰लक। तब किसान अपन्ना जी मैँ बिचार॰लक, ई सभ कै किछु कर कै देखाइ दी, तब आही जे किछु समुझ जाय। एक दीन ज अपन्ना बेटा कै बजौलक, आओर कह॰लक जे, थोर लक॰री हम॰रठ सामन्ने ले आवठ। ज, लक॰री कै उन्ह॰का साम॰ने एक रस॰री सँ सकत सँ बान्ह॰लक। फेर सभ सँ कह॰लक जे रस्सी जन खोलन्ही आओर लक॰री कै तोरि डालठ। तब सभ मील कै जोर कैल॰खिन, मुदा किछु ने भेले। फेर किसान खोल कै एक एक गो लक॰री देलक जेक॰रा के ज सभ

झटऽपट तोरि डललन्का। तब उन्हऽकर बाप कहऽलक जे, ए बेटा, जे तोँ बान्हल लकऽरी के तरह से आपुस मेँ मीलल रहऽ, तऽ सभ दुसऽमन के दाँत खट्टा करऽबे ; आओर जब छिरिया गेलै तऽ जनिहऽ जे बिगर गेलै। जे छिरियाएल, से बिगऽरल।

छठम बात।

हुँड़ार आओर भेँड़ा केर मेल।

एक बेर हुँड़ार सभ भेँड़ा सभ से कहऽलाइ भेजलऽकै जे, आवौँ, हमँ तोँहँ अपऽना मेँ मेल करी। किये अपन्ना मेँ लरी, आओर एक दोसऽरा केर लेहू केर पियासल रही। ई पाजी कुत्ता बीलऽकुल लराइ के जर छिकै। इनाहिँ हरऽदम भूक भूक कै हमऽरा भड़कबैथऽ आओर हमऽरा तोहऽरा सैँ लरऽबैथऽ। ओकऽरा सभ हमऽरा भीर भेज दे, फेर किये झगऽरा एत। हमऽरा तोहऽरा मेँ सदाय प्यार आओर मेल रहत। तब तोहर बारो * नहिँ भिगऽतौ। गँवार भेँड़ा ई मटऽखठ हुँड़ार सभ के बात मनलऽकै आओर कुत्ता सभ कै हुँड़ार केर पास पठाइ देलऽकै। पहिले तै हुँड़ार सभ कुत्ता सभ कै खा गेल, फेर भेँड़ा सभ के पाछे चक्कुर भार कै परल आओर थोर के दीन मेँ सभ कै डकार कर गेलै। साँच है, बैरी धोखा देयऽ; जे बर गँवार छिका जे ओकऽरा सच्चा समुझऽ॥

सातम बात।

बाघ आओर हुँड़ार आओर चीता।

एक बेर बाघ आओर हुँड़ार आओर चीता आपुस मेँ ई ठहऽरौलन्का जे, हम सभ मील कै सिकार मारी। फेर अपन्ना मेँ बाँटि ली। ई ठानि कै जङ्गल मेँ कूद फान करै लगऽन्हा, आओर जब एक बड़ऽका ठो करिया हरीन मारलऽन्का, तब बाघ बाजल जे आवऽ एकऽरा के बाँटी, आओर झट ओकऽरा तीन टुकऽरा कर डालक, आओर गरज के बजलऽकै जे, पहिल टुकऽरा तै हमँ लेब, किये हमँ जङ्गल केर राजा छिकौँ, आओर दोसऽरो † हमऽहीँ ‡ लेब, किये हमँ एकऽरा के मारऽला मेँ बर दौर धूप करऽलौँ है,

---

* Emphatic for बार, 'even a hair.'

† Emphatic for दोसर, 'the second also.'

‡ Emphatic for हमँ, 'I myself.'

आओर तेसर हुकऽरा ई धरल एहै, देखी तै जे किन्हऽकर मुँह छिकन्ह जे हमऽरा सामऽना सैँ ले जैता। ई सुन कै चीता आओर ऊँड़ार लँगऽरी दबाइ कै भागल, आओर बाघ हरीन कै एकऽसरे चट कैलक। ई कहावत साँच है, जेकर लाठी तेकर भैँस ॥

आठम बात।

माँटी आउर पीतर केर घैला के बातऽचीत।

एक बेर कहइँ नद्दी बहल। तब एक पीतर केर घैला, आओर एगो माँटी के घैला बहल। तब पीतर के घैला माँटी केर घैला से कहलऽकै जे, हमऽरा सङ्ग लागल चलऽ, तब हमेँ तोहऽरा बचाइ लेबौ। माँटी केर घैला बाजल जे, ई आइस बर नानू बात करऽलौँ हमेँ अपऽना केर भल मानब आओर सदाय गुन गबैत रहब; मुदा साँच पूछौ, तै हमऽरा ई डर छिकै जे कहइँ पानि केर लहर केर धक्का सैँ आइस केर लग नै जाइ रही; किये कि जे आइस सैँ दूरे रहब, तै एनाही हिलैत डोलैत कहइँ किनार पर जाइ लागब, मुदा जे आइस सैँ भैँठ भेल, आओर कहइँ भुलऽला सैँ ठोकर लागल, तब हमरठ पेठ फाटि जाएत। साँच है, बरऽका सभ से आस रक्खौ, मुदा सगे नहिँ जाए ॥

नौअम बात।

एक मुनऽसी बजार मेँ बैसल चिट्ठी लिखैछला। एक बिदेसी आएल, आओर बाजल जे, मुनऽसी जी, की लिखैछी। मुनऽसी जी जवाब देलऽखिन्ह जे, भैया चिट्ठी लिखैछी। तब उ कहलऽकन्ह जे, हमऽरो सलाम लिख देब। मुनऽसी जी कहलऽखिन्ह जे नहिँ जी, अरऽजी लिखैछी। तब उ कहलऽकन्ह जे, हमऽरो सही कर देब। मुनऽसी जी औकऽताइ कै बजलऽथिन्ह जे, तमस्सुक लिखैछी। तब उ बाजल जे, हमऽरो गोवाही लिख देब। मुनऽसी जी सोचलऽका जे, ई तै कोइ अजब ढङ्ग केर आदिमी देख परैयठ। पुछलऽखिन्ह जे, तोहर नाम की छिक। तब उ हँसल, आओर बाजल जे, हमर नाम छिक मानौँ नै मानौँ, हमेँ तोहर पाऊन ॥

दसम बात।

कोइ बरा आदिमी केर घर मेँ रात के सभे आगि लागल। उ तो अप्पन बाल बच्चा समेत निकस भागल। नोकर सभ कैँ हुकुम देलक, जे, चीज बस्तु निकासौँ। एतऽना मेँ आगि बढ़ल

भरक गेल ; सारा घर धुआँ धार हो गेल । नोकर बाजल जे, हम की की निकामौं, सब ज बर अद्मिी कहय उठऽला आओर कहलऽथिन्ह जे, बाबा, झोँपऽरा आगि लागे, सब के निकऽसे से लाभ ॥

एगारऽहम बात ।

गँवार गोआरिनि ।

एगो गँवारि * गोआरिनि माथा पर दहेरी धैले चलल आइरहैयऽ। चलैत चलैत ओकऽरा जी मेँ ई उमङ्ग उठऽलै जे, ई दही के बेँचब, पैसा सैँ आम मोल लेब ; किछु आम हमऽरा जौरे अब, सभ मिलाइ कै तीन से सैँ किछु बढि आइत। ओकऽरा मेँ सैँ किछु सरि पचि जाइत ; तब हुँ, अढ़ाइ से ते बचऽबे। आओर ओहि मेँ से जे बचत ओकर बेसी दाम मोलत। तब दिवारी मेँ एक हरिअर सारी लेब। हौँ, हौँ, हरिअर सारी हमऽरा मुँह पर नीक खुलत। आओर बस, हम ते हरिअरे सारी लेब ; आओर ओकऽरा पेहन कै मेला जाएब ; आओर मुखऽरा केर चमक झलक देखाएब, आओर ऐँठ अौँठ कै चलैत चलैत मेँ सै से लचऽकत चलब। एहि सोच बिचार मेँ ज गँवारि गोआरिनि जे किछु चमक ठमक कै टेढ़ चाल चलल, तब दहेरी ओकऽरा माथा पर सैँ गिर कै चूर चूर हो गेलै, आओर सौँसो बनल बनाएल घर बिगर गेलै ॥

बारऽहम बात ।

चील्ह आओर कौआ ।

एक चील्ह के चोँच मेँ घोँघा रहै। केतऽनौ † करऽतो पर फऽकलक, तैँ घोँघा ने फुटऽलै। तब एक कौआ ई राह बतौलऽकै जे, ई घोँघा कै चोँच मेँ लै कै बडुत ऊपर उर आ, आओर उहाँ से गिराइ दे, तब घोँघा फूट आइत। चील्ह कहऽलक जे ई बात बर नीक बतौलै, आओर घोँघा कै लै कै उरल, आओर खूब ऊपर जाइ कै हारि

* Fem. of गँवार.

† Emphatic for केतऽना, 'however much.'

देलक। ओनाहिँ घोँघा धरऽती पर गिरल, टुकऽरा टुकऽरा भै गेल, आओर कौआ ओकर गूदा खा लेलक। तनियक मेँ चील्ह नीचा उतऽरल, तब छिलुका छार के आओर किछु ने पौलक॥

तेरऽहम बात।

खट्टा अँगूर।

एक खिखिर कोइ बाग मेँ जाइ निकऽसल, देखलऽकै जे अँगूर के ऐसन गुच्छा पाकल टाटी मेँ लटऽकल छिकै, कि जेकऽरा से रस चुऐत रहैयऽ, आओर कोइ रखऽवारो नहिँ रहै। ई देख कै ओकऽरा मुँह मेँ पानि भर ऐलै। ऊ बड़त तरहेँ उछऽलल कूदल मुदा अँगुर के थौका तक नहिँ चुम्हऽलक। जब कोइ उपाय से दाव नऽ लागल ओनाहिँ बरऽबराइत भेल उहाँ से चलल, जे खट्टा अँगूर के खाय॥

चौदऽहम बात।

रसाइनी।

एक रसाइनी कोइ अदिमी से कहऽलक जे, जोँ तोँ किछु चानी हमऽरा पास लै आवौँ तोँ हम एक ऐसन जड़ी मिलाइ दी जे तुरन्त ही ऊ चानी से सोना होइ जाए। ऊ सीधा साधा अदिमी ओकऽरा पटी मेँ आ गेल, आओर कहइँ से दुख सुख सहि कै दू से रुपैया के चानी ऊ रसाइनी कै ला देलऽकै। रसाइनी ओही* रात कै अप्पन बिस्तर उठाइ कै कहइँ चलल गेलै। तब ऊ बेचारा बिपत केर मारल ओहि बड़ुट रसाइनी के खोज मेँ दौर धुप करैँ लागल, जङ्गल जङ्गल छान लेलक, तैँओ ऊ रसाइनी के पता कहइँ नहिँ लगऽलै। ओकऽरा ऐसने घबऽराएल देख कर, एक अदिमी कहलऽकै जे, तोरा से ई भूल भेलौ, कि वैसन बड़ुट अतीथ के फाँदा मेँ फस गेलै। परन्तु अब पछऽतौला आओर ओकऽरा खोज मेँ दौर धूप करऽला सैँ किछु नहिँ होतौक। तोहऽरा एक बात सुनवैछी जेकऽरा सदाय इआद राखल चाही॥

---

* Emphatic for ओइ, 'on that very night.'

पनरहम बात।

एक चिरईं कोइ किसान के बाग मेँ जाइ कै काँच पाकल फल सभ केर सभ काटि जाइत रहैथइ किसान सदाय ओकरा खोज मेँ रहैहल। एक दीन अँगूर केर टाटी पर जाल लगाइ कै ओकरा घेलक, आओर मारै लेल चहलक। चिरईं किसान से कहलक जे, जौँ तोँ हमरा छाड़ि देबै, तोँ हमेँ ई भलाइ केर बदला तोहरा कै एक बात बतौबौँ, जेहि मेँ तोहरा बड़ लाभ होतौ। किसान कहलक जे, तोँ पहिले बताइ दे तब हमेँ तोहरा छाड़ि देबौ। चिरईं ओकरा तीन बात कहलकै, एक तै ई जे, बैरी जे अपना बस मेँ आ जाए, तकरा छाड़ल नहिँ चाही, दोसर जे बात धेआन मेँ नहिँ आवे, ओकरा नहिँ मानै कै चाही, तेसर गेल चीज केर लेल पछतावै कै नहिँ चाही। चौठ एक बात आओर एछ। जब तोँ हमरा छाड़ि देबै तब हम कह देबौ। किसान ई बात कैँ सुन कै जेसन कहलक रहै तेहनहिँ कैलक, आओर ओहि चिरईं कै छाड़ि देलक। तब चिरईं भीत पर बैस कै बाजल जे, हमरा पेट मेँ मुरगी केर अण्डौ* सेँ बड़ एक मोती रहै, जौँ तोँ हमरा नहिँ छाड़ितै आओर मारि दहतै, तोँ ऊ मोती तोहरा हाथ लगितइ। किसान पछतावै लागल। ऊ कहलक जे, रे गँवार तोँ हमर तीनो बात तुरन्ते† भूल गेलै; किये कि हमेँ तोहर बैरी रहौँ, जब धैल रहै, तब किहे छाड़लै; आओर मुरगी केर बरौबर तै हमहोँ नहिँ छी, फेर मुरगी केर आँड़ा से बड़ कै मोती हमरा पेट मेँ होएब कब धेआन मेँ आ सकैयइ, पर तोँ एहि पर भरोसा करलक, आओर जब हमेँ तोहरा हाथ से निकस गेलौँ, तब पछतौला से की होतौ। एहि से ई फल निकलल, जे पहिले से सभ काम कै बड़त सोच बिचार करै कै चाही, आओर जब कोइ काम बिगर जाए, तब फेर पछतावै के नहिँ चाही॥

सोरहम बात।

कोइ बनिक कै दू लरिका रहय। जब उन्हकर बाप मरलथ, तब दुओ भाइ उन्हकर धन आपुस मेँ बाँटि लेलन्हा। बड़ भाइ अपन रुपैया ढेबुआ सुख चैन आओर खेल तमासा मेँ उड़ावै लागल, आओर छोटा भाइ बड़ा जतन से बनौज बेपार करै लागल। एक दीन बड़ भाइ छोटा भाइ केर उलहन्ना दे कै कहलक जे, ए भाइ,

* Emphatic for अण्डा, 'even an egg.'

† Emphatic for तुरन्त.

किये दीन भर अनाज किसक तौलैत रहैछे ; हमऽरा बड़े रहऽ, खा पीय, चैन करऽ। बऽन दीन केर पाछाँ, जब छोटा भाइ लेनाइ देनाइ से बऊत रुपैया एकट्ठा कर लेलक, तब ओकर बर भाइ, जे राग रङ्ग खेल तमासा मेँ अपन सभ धन उड़ाइ भिखारी होइ गेल रहै, ओकऽरा डेओढ़ी पर आइ कै कहै लागल जे, ए भैया, हमैँ तोहऽरा ठट्ठा मेँ छोरौले रहौँ। परन्तु जौँ हमऽहूँ तोहऽरे नाहित बनीज बेपार करऽतौँ, आओर अनाज तौलऽतौँ, तौँ आज पौ भर अनाज दूसे उसे से माँगि कै नहिँ खेतौँ। साँच है अलऽसी ऐसऽने कीरा छिक, जे धन कै धूर कर डलैयऽ।

सतरऽहम बात।

लालऽची कुत्ता।

कोइ कुत्ता नदी के तीर पर एक हड्डी पौलक आओर मुँह मेँ लेलक। जबऽहौँ फरऽछाँहौँ ओकर पानि मेँ देखऽलक तबऽहौँ समुझऽलक जे दोसर हड्डी छिक। मारे लालच के मुँह खोलऽलक, के ओकऽरौ के पानि से निकास ली। तऽ ज हड्डी जे मुँह मेँ रहै सेहो खोलक। साँच है, लालच से माँछी दूध पर बैसल, पाँख लपटा गेलै। दूनो हाथ मलै आओर माँथा धूनै लागल, जे लालऽची बुरा बलाय।

Reg. No. 7502J—510—28-8-85.